South Asia: Nation Building and Federalism

South Asia: Nation Building and Federalism

Editors

Lok Raj Baral

&

Krishna Hachhethu

Vij Books India Pvt Ltd
New Delhi (India)

Published by

Vij Books India Pvt Ltd
(Publishers, Distributors & Importers)
2/19, Ansari Road
Delhi – 110 002
Phones: 91-11-43596460, 91-11-47340674
Fax: 91-11-47340674
e-mail: vijbooks@rediffmail.com

Copyright © 2014, Nepal Center for Contemporary Studies, Kathmandu, Nepal

First Published in India: 2014

ISBN: 978-93-82652-27-4

Contents

Contents

Introduction

Lok Raj Baral and Krishna Hachhethu

South Asia is a region having heterogeneous characteristics of its member states. Management of social diversity has continued to remain a big question confronting each country of this region. Of two competing models of nation building – nation-states and state-nations – the former seems dominant in South Asia. "Nation-states tend to be assimilationist in character. Removal of ethnic and cultural diversities is one of the key features of nation-states. In contrast, state-nation policies work on two levels: creation of a sense of belonging with respect to the larger political community, while simultaneously putting in place institutional guarantees for safeguarding politically salient diversities, such as language, religion and culturally sacred norms" (Varshney, 2013: 46). The dominant path of nation building in the South Asian countries, as stated by Phandis and Ganguli, is, " post-colonial nation building approaches focused almost exclusively on creating a unified 'national identity' based around either common political values and citizenship or a putative majoritarian ethnic identity" (2001: 13).

In the formative phase of modern state in the post-colonial era, most South Asian countries adopted democracy, socialism, secularism and nationalism as the four pillars of nation building in their respective countries. Ethnicity, minority rights and inclusion were almost ignored in management of macro politics. India could be an exception to some extent as the post-colonial Indian politics intakes some inclusive measures, i.e. formation of federal units primarily on the basis of linguistic identity, reservation for schedule castes and tribes, preferential rights to the native people in some states of North-east and Kashmir etc. Other South Asian countries failed to uphold some of above mentioned four pillars of nation building. Nepal, Bangladesh and Pakistan had common trajectory of political development, altering democracy by dictatorship vis versa. Indian and Sri Lanka have retained democracy without any interruption, but Sri Lanka gave up the principle of secularism. Bangladesh and Pakistan also diverted from being secular to Islamic states. So in South Asia, nation building was largely a state designed project of assimilating minorities into the fold of the majority or dominant group's value system. For instance Nepal, since the time of its unification in 1769, the rulers had tried to develop Nepal as a homogeneous, monolithic and unitary state providing protection to one religion (Hindu), one language (Nepali) and one caste group (hill Brahmin-Chhetri), ignoring the reality of diversified and pluralistic character of Nepali society. 'One language, one nation' and 'one state, one religion' (i.e. Hindu Nepal, Islamic Pakistan, Bangladesh and Maldives, Buddhist Bhutan and Sri Lanka) indicated the old model of nation building adopted in South Asia. Incongruous of such assimilative model of nation building for a pluralistic society is manifested in various ways. Rise of ethnicity and regionalism in Nepal, Tamil insurgency in Sri Lanka, Chakma revolt in Bangladesh, dissent against Panjabi's domination in Pakistani politics, ethnic conflicts in North-east India, all these are evidences of posing challenges against the prevalent model of nation building in South Asian countries.

India and Pakistan have adopted federal system from the very beginning; the rest remain unitary states. At the formative phase, both India and Pakistan seemed federal more in appearance but unitary in essence. Recurrence of military rule in Pakistan ever since its birth has obstructed the federal system to evolve on its natural course. Now, provinces of Pakistan are more powerful than before. Federating India has become possible only since the end of one party Congress dominant system and the rise of ethnic and regional parties as balancer in coalition politics at the centre. Now, one could observe a paradigm shift in the nation building process in India and Pakistan. A shift from assimilation to accommodation of minorities has taken place. Nepal is now embarking on a federal system. A new Nepal with federal character is expected to bring a change in nation building model of Nepal. Assimilation of minorities into the dominant hill high Hindu castes' culture needs to be changed by accommodation of social diversity. Bangladesh, being a unitary state and largely homogeneous society, has a constitutional arrangement for the protection of rights of Hindu minority and Chakma Hill Tribes. A successful military suppression of the Liberation Tiger of Tamil Eelam (LTTE) does not mean death of Tamil's aspiration if the Sri Lankan rulers do not take steps to assuage the feeling of the Tamil population. Whether or not the countries that have adopted unitary system can manage the emergent crisis is a different matter.

Nepal Centre for Contemporary Studies (NCCS)'s seminar organized in August 2012 has tried to dwell upon the broad theme of nation building in South Asia with special references of the countries of the region. Some scholars of South Asia have raised the problems and issues that confront them. However, by way of caution, it must be admitted that only few countries are federal. Nepal, a new candidate for federalism, has theoretically accepted federalism as one of the means of nation building. The titles of papers indicate the various experiences of each country. **Multiple Paths to Nation Building in South Asia** tries to introduce the theme in general. The author (Lok Raj Baral) thus takes a holistic approach to nation building. Three signposts of nation building, as illustrated by Baral, are: democracy with political stability, diversity with accommodation, and economic development with empowerment of the disadvantaged sections of society. Some other thoughts of emphasis are: the concept of state building and nation building overlaps in their attributes; political instability and crisis of governance contributes negatively to nation building; the politics of regionalism and ethnicity has added new dimensions in politics of the region; demand for inclusiveness and empowerment have widened the arenas of nation building; and secular values are the hallmarks of the modern nation state.

Concerning the form of government, South Asia presents two different models, federal and unitary, of nation building. India and Pakistan have adopted federal model since their independence in 1947. In his article – **India's Federalism and Practice of Politics: Challenges and Possibilities**, Bishnu N. Mohapatra analyses two parts of India's federalism. One is about construction of federal units primarily on the basis of language based ethnic identity to respect a vast diversity of Indian society. The logic behind such construction is to balance the "imperative of national unity with the claims of regional and linguistic diversities in India". So far the centre-state relation – another dimension of this paper – is concerned; Mohapatra explains the reason behind evolution of Indian federalism in a direction different from the time of its architect.

Constitutionally, India has adopted a centralized federalism with its desire for building a strong nation-state but practically it has evolved towards a decentralized federalism. The gap between constitutional arrangement and actual course of Indian federalism is well captured by the author. "There are four elements of the present conjuncture that influence the federal governance in India: the ongoing process of economic liberalization, the emergence of coalitional politics at the centre and regionalization of politics and finally the continuing presence of exclusivist nationalism".

Pakistan is an example of a static federalism. The numbers of its federal units remain the same i.e. four provinces (Punjab, Sindh, Balochistan and North-West Frontier Province , recently renamed Khyber Pakhtunkhwa, as designed at time of its independence whereas India's federal units have increased from 12 to 28 as of today.   But the 18th amendment to the Pakistan constitution is acclaimed by Ayesha Siddiqa in her article **Re-imagining Pakistan: Identity Politics in a National Security State** as an entry point for greater regional autonomy and recognition of ethnicity as political constituency in federal arrangement. There is a demand for more provinces, i.e. a province for Mohajirs, Pushtoon province in Balochistan, Saraiki province in South Punjab, Hazara province in North Punjab and Bahawalpur in Punjab. Demands for these new provinces have come up in account of dissension on ethnic and regional economic disparity in the existing provinces. But there is strong resistance against these demands by a dominant group, Punjabi, which has stronghold in army, bureaucracy and national politics. Taking this into account, Ayesha concludes that "provincial autonomy may be an uphill task, but ethnic autonomy is even harder because the power elite of Pakistan is not primed to accept the concept".

Bangladesh and Sri Lanka are in common in taking unitary model of nation building, despite different trajectories of ethnic conflict persisting in them. A unitary state cannot offer more than self-government based on decentralization, devolution and autonomy. Abdur Rob Khan in his article, **CHT Regional Council: Regional Autonomy within Unitary System of Bangladesh**, gives a picture of duality of local government in Bangladesh: formally it is constructed on the basis of decentralization system but practically it operates in centralized way. CHT regional council is a different innovation and an outcome of 20 years insurgency waged by native people of Chittagong Hill Tract. They are distinct ethnic groups, different from the dominant Bengali community. An attempt to imposing Bengali language and culture over non-Bengali population produced a violent ethnic conflict which eventually produced a Peace Accord in 1997 with a provision of a political arrangement – a regional council – for hill people residing in Chittagong Hill Tract whose language and culture is different from Bengali. Khan alerts that non-compliance of other significant provisions of the Peace Accord, i.e. rehabilitation of refugees, sorting out of land disputes and demilitarization of the CHT etc. may lead to re-invite violent confrontation between the government of Bangladesh and tribe of CHT.

Ethnic conflict in Sri Lanka, another unitary state of South Asia, has recently landed with a military victory over LTTE. But the cause of civil war between Sinhala majority and Tamil minority remains intact. Rohan Edrisinha in his article, **The Federal Debate in Sri Lanka**, states that federalism as an idea to address the diversity and division of the Sri Lankan society has long been persisted. Thirteen Amendments to the Sri Lankan constitution with its provision of power devolution could be an entry point towards a journey of transforming Sri Lanka into a federal state. But the rise of Sinhala majoritarianism on the one hand and the LTTE's assertion for separation of North-east (Tamil dominated area) on the other did not allow an amicable solution of violent ethnic conflicts of the country. For a way out in the future, Edrisinha gives a thought: "Though Sri Lanka may have entered a post-war period; it has not entered a post-conflict period as the underlying causes of the conflict remain". Hence the need, therefore, for far reaching constitutional and political reform that should include substantial devolution of powers and possibly a federal constitution".

What lessons Nepal can learn from South Asian experiences of nation building. Obviously there are two paths, unitary as adopted by Bangladesh and Sri Lanka and federal as taken by Indian and Pakistan. Nepal is a country of social diversity as it is the home of around 125 caste/ethnic and linguistic groups and of 10 religious communities. The present state of ethnic conflicts in Nepal – dominant hill high castes versus excluded indigenous nationalities (popularly known as Juniata) and dominated Parade versus discriminated Mahesh – is largely a product of the past faulty assimilative model of nation building. Because the old model of nation building in Nepal has produced an inequality among the social groups. The country has, therefore, recently realized a need of transformation to a federal state. **Federalism Discourse in Nepal: An Appraisal**, written by Krishna P. Khanal, gives a glimpse of the evolution of federal discourse in Nepal in four phases: its genesis with introduction of democracy in 1950, revival of federal demand with restoration of multiparty system in 1990, proposal of federal Nepal as an integral part of the post April 2006 Jana Angolan It's agenda of restructuring the Nepali state, and negotiation for designing federal Nepal under the First Constituent Assembly (2008-2012). The expiry of the Constituent Assembly without producing a new constitution has halted the federal design but is likely to resume after the election of the Second Constituent Assembly, schedule for 19 November 2013.

Krishna Hachhethu's paper, **Ethnic Conflict and Federalism in Nepal,** focuses on division of Nepali society and politics on model of federalism to be adopted in Nepal. The dominant group, hill high castes, and the traditional political parties, i.e. Nepali Congress and Communist Party of Nepal (Unified Marxist-Leninist or UML) are in favour of territorial federalism. Other pole, newly mobilized social groups, i.e. Janajati and Madheshi and political forces that emerged from the last Constituent Assembly election, i.e. Unified Communist Party of Nepal (Maoist), Madhesh- based regional parties and Indigenous Peoples' Caucus Group stand for identity- based federalism, if not ethnic federalism. What differences lie between the proposed two models, territorial and identity based federalism? Territorial based federalism – attributed with a recommendation of few provinces (5-7 provinces), non-ethnic name of provinces and vertical demarcation of provincial boundaries combining all ecological zones (mountain, hill and Tarai) – suits best to retain nation building of Nepal along the line with the concept of nation-states. Whereas identity based federalism – featured with a suggestion of 10-14 provinces, ethnic name of provinces, and reinvention of ethno-political territory while delaminating provincial boundary – follows a model of state-nations. To explore the middle ground between such two antagonistic proposals, Hachhethu gives a thought: "Restructuring the Nepali state with inclusive polity and federal design is acclaimed, particularly by Janajatis and Madheshis, as a remedy of long standing ethnic problems of the country. But if the federal Nepal is not crafted well and managed properly, it could be a journey towards a danger zone. No doubt, federal Nepal under designing should address the problems of exclusion; it, at the same time, should accommodative the different and conflicting interest of diverse social groups so that people belonging to different segments of society could feel a sense of their ownership in new federal Nepal".

The comparative experiences of nation building in South Asia prove that the assimilative model is not appropriate. Had not India balanced both the ethnicity building and nation building through its own federal design, it would have been difficult to retain integration of such a vast diversified country. Pakistan also recognizes ethnicity as political constituency in its formal federal political arrangement, nevertheless the absent of autonomy to federal units has created a challenge for its integration. Siddiqa recalls, "The lack of provincial autonomy during the 1960s had led to circumstances that propelled the dismemberment of East Pakistan in 1971". In the case of Sri Lanka, Edrisinha is of the opinion that the rise of Sinhalese majoritarianism that incorporated in political and constitutional arrangement, i.e. replacing secularism by Buddhism and making Sinhala as the only official language of the country, has produced bacteria of national disintegration. Bangladesh's attempt to impose Bengali nationalism over non-Bengali population of the country produced an ethnic insurgency in CHT. Here, we can see a valid logic, argued by Khanal, for transforming Nepal into a federal state for political management of social diversity so as to minimize the conflicts emanating from diversities. Hachhethu sees both ethnic and territorial federalism as extreme proposals as the country specific context of Nepal demands identity based federalism as an appropriate measure to put conflicting social groups into a broad federal Nepal. All these arguments follow the major thrust of Baral's paper that "Now country with diversity becomes a nation when it accepts unity in diversity".

References

Phandis, Urmila and Rajat Ganguly. 2001. Ethnicity and Nation Building in South Asia. New Delhi: Sage Publication.

Varshney, Ashutosh. 2013. "How has India Federalism Done?". Studies in Indian Politics. Vol. 1, No.1.

Multiple Paths to Nation Building in South Asia

Lok Raj Baral

I

Understanding Nation-State and Nation Building

South Asian states have not yet become full-fledged nation states. Many are new constructs, despite their 'givens' or old common civilization links and historical connectivity. Afghanis, Nepalis, Indians, Sri Lankan, Pakistanis, Bangladeshis , Bhutanese and the Maldivians , are peoples who came from diverse races and tribes or other social categories to form nations and states .Common language, culture, defined territory and other identities are specific to the peoples forming a nation. It is more an emotional or psychological feeling that "joins and differentiates it, in the subconscious conviction of its members from other people in almost vital way". So "defining and conceptualizing the nation is more difficult because the essence of a nation is intangible". [1] The emerging trends have also shed new light on defining and shaping the nation and state or nation-state as the ideology of nationalism is being subsumed by the emphasis placed on sub-national constructs such as subaltern groups and ethnicity. It is also being realized that in countries with deep ethnic, linguistic, regional and religious divisions, nation states as they were defined and constructed are no more relevant to the new aspirations of people hitherto living within identifiable national borders. And reasons for such dramatic shift in orientations of people can be attributed to the failure of 'nation building'. Nevertheless, one or two denominator cannot provide us with a full picture of nation building. It is as much related to variables and culture of developing a feeling of togetherness owning the defined territory and respective identity of diverse people living within a country. Now country with diversity becomes a nation when it accepts "unity in diversity". In a

---

1 Walker Connor ," A National is a Nation, is a State, is an Ethnic Group ..." in John Hutchinson & Anthony D. Smith, eds., *Nationalism* , Oxford: Oxford University Press, 1994),p.20

country like China, it is less problematic because of the homogeneous Han population (92 percent); though simmering and sometimes open discontent of some minority communities are also evident in recent years. China's Muslim minority population of the province of Xinjiang[2], which borders with Afghanistan, "might be dangerously affected by the developments across the border.

It is also remarkable that the trends of globalization, cross-country and in-country terrorism and insurgencies, international division of labour, migrations have moderated the feeling of radical nationalism. Political parties that have had tried to find their sustenance in xenophobia are finding difficulty to use this instrument for mobilizing people. American involvement in Afghanistan and use of Pakistan as a conduit for its operations against the Mujahidin despite Pakistan's grumbling against the former, have stirred the Pakistani sentiments against the American but it has not been able to extricate itself fully from the cobweb of external penetration and incursions. So is the case of Nepal, a country having deep and extensive relations with India. Some politicians and intellectual elites who talk of infringement of national independence and sovereignty can hardly provide any alternative model of Nepal's relations with India. Some are of the opinion that Nepal's landlocked situation, too much dependence on India, open border are some of the hurdles for developing Nepal's own personality as a nation state. However, how far such presumptions reflect the reality needs to be examined objectively.

The multiple paths to nation building or nation-state building or "national state"[3] building in South Asia cannot be examined in isolation. Country's society, composition of population, ethnic conditions, aspirations, political system , policies and strategies adopted by the state, capacity to manage diversity, inclusiveness with empowerment of diverse sections of society constitute the elements of nation building. Here we must

---

2 Shlomo Ben-Ami, " China's Afghan Game Plan", reproduced in *the Kathmandu Post*, July 9,2012,p.36

3 See T.K.Oommen, " Evolving Inclusive Societies through Constitutions: The Case of Nepal" (An Unpublished paper presented at a Seminar on Social Inclusion Policies in South Asian States" (Kathmandu, CNAS, 25-27 June 2009. According Oommen, the nation state has the characteristics of being assimilationist I, e. it tries to impose some sort of uniform culture, language and religion. It is thus opposed to the separate identity of each ethnic communities living within a country. National state as conceived by him accept diversities.

also be clear that both state and nation building are inextricable parts of each other, for state building also includes the elements of nation building. Faced with the problem of making the two –state and nation, both the concepts have been conjoined by the Western scholars. Nation reflects the emotional and cultural aspects of citizens, while state is more or less a secular connotation that is related to organization of state- sponsored institutions and processes. Since the classical definition of state entails four elements –sovereignty, population, territory and government--, it tries to provide us with a narrative of nation building as well. Any nation that involves its people as fully sovereign by enabling them to make their own constitution with which modern state runs its system reflects the doctrine of popular sovereignty. In authoritarian and totalitarian states or in traditional monarchical states, people are merely used mechanically showing rather wrongly that such regimes are based on people.

In actual practice, however, power enjoyed by the authoritarian rulers is not legitimized by the free will of the people. The traditional monarchy of Nepal got its longevity unless the people revolted against it in 2006 or unless it could resist the pressure of popular discontent through the means of coercion and manipulation. If one goes by Max Weber's three-fold characteristics of legitimacy, monarchy had traditional legitimacy based on religion, tradition and indoctrination of people by the falsified notion of symbol of unity and territorial integrity of the nation. In other words, monarchs were perceived as the incarnation of god by ordinary Nepalis, whereas some educated people also saw them as the symbol of national unity and stability. Both the myths, however, exploded when the people accepted the end of monarchy without any fuss.

A state is theoretically sovereign despite being traditional or authoritarian. Sovereignty is thus a neutral word in dealing with the pure theory of the state. The Soviet Union tried to be a nation state by force, not by willingness of its people. It crumbled when its pretentious ideology of communism failed to cope with the new challenges posed by its own internal contradictions, corruption, rustic state structures and unrealistic competition for being hegemonic power at par with the United States. Pakistan has a traumatic trajectory of political development that eventually led to the disintegration of the country itself. The Bengali nationalism and Islamic ideological orientation of elites of West Pakistan could not be reconciled. Baluchistan that borders Afghanistan is in perennial conflict with the centralized state structure as the Baluch aspiration is unpalatable for the power elites of Pakistan. So is the case with the Sind where the Mohajir community is not at ease with the rest.

The second element of the state- people- has many things to do with the 'nation building process. Popular sovereignty which is basically a rule by the people has a wider meaning and spirit. State without being the representative of popular sentiments does not only fail to rule but also tend to weaken the nation building processes. People not only produce government through the instrument of periodical elections, but also identify themselves with the overall development of the country. Governance to be effective and broad-based must enjoy the confidence of all sections of society.

It can be generalized that the emotional integration is still far off in many countries of South Asia. Even those countries which are relatively better in index of nation- state building, have not secured the desired level of integration. Many are riddled with conflict, trends of secession or with the rising demands for more autonomy and self and shared rule. India and Sri Lanka, the two models of democracy in South Asia, are still undergoing the stresses and strains of national integration. India has all along been embroiled in Kashmir and in the Northeast since independence. Yet, to the credit of Indian political system and resilient approach of Indian power elites, it has been partly successful in either managing nation building process or in containing crises. It is to the advantage of India that separatist trends and insurgencies do not spread in other parts of India. They are localized. It has helped a lot for keeping the integrity of Indian nation. The Maoist insurgency seems to be exception as it has spread over more than 120 districts in India and to which the Indian Prime Minister, Manmohan Singh, has termed it as the greatest menace to Indian security. Its root cause is attributed to extreme poverty precipitated by the failure of the state machinery to cater the minimum services to the needy section of population. So development that entails all the ingredients of social justice including poverty eradication is related to people of a nation state. However, this issue cannot be emotionally linked to the larger context of nation building, although redressing the hardships of citizens is very much central to the function of state.

Today, 'nation' (imagined?) without territory remains a sentiment only. The Palestinians have been struggling to find a defined territorial nation state. Although Palestine has been recognized by the United Nations as a nation, aspiration of people there is to realize a territorial Palestine homeland. Nations fight for territories even if such territories do not matter in actual life of the people. The barren land where even the cattle do not find a blade of grass has become the most disputed issue in inter-state relations. China and India or India and Pakistan are in perpetual conflict for the ownership of lands in the glaciers of the Himalayas. Nepalis are still nostalgic about the loss of territories captured by them during the Anglo-Nepal War in 1814-15. These territories were extended to the Teesta river to the East and Kumaon and Garhwal to the West. Nepalese lost these territories to the British-India government in the Treaty of Sugauli. Later, the districts of Western Tarai—Banke, Bardia, Kailali and Kanchanpur --- were returned to Nepal as a good will to Nepal in 1860. Since then, Nepal has a stable international border stretching from Mechi (East) to the Mahakali (West) rivers, and from the northern Tibetan border to the Tarai abutting the five provinces of India—West Bengal, Sikkim, Bihar, Uttar Pradesh and Uttarakhand. Small border dispute is a regular feature in Nepal-India relations, though no serious border conflict has ever arisen as it happened to India and China. These two countries went to short border war in 1962 but China soon stopped it after what it called "teaching a lesson to India". Although the border conflict persists even today, the two have been able to maintain peace along the entire Sino-Indian border despite provocative gestures shown from time to time. In 1971, China threatened to open a front by way of extending support to the beleaguered Pakistani military ruler, then in war with India. Pakistan wanted that China, being a good ally, open a war front for harassing India. When that didn't happen, Pakistani military ruler and other politicians were demoralized. China in fact did only try to boost the sagging morale of Pakistani rulers but had no intention of involving itself in the India-Pakistan war. It seems that both India and China are not likely to enter into another phase of war because of the changed regional and global context of power politics.

How emotional integration is the most important factor for maintaining the territorial integrity of a country had been demonstrated by the disintegration of Pakistan in 1971. The Bengali nationalism was hurt in 1948 when the Father of the Nation, Mohammad Ali Jinnah, spoke in Dhaka saying that the Urdu would be the national language of Pakistan. Language issue sowed the seeds of separatism, although other factors such as economic disparity between the East and the West, disproportionate of power distribution, distrust between the two wings, to mention a few were responsible for alienation of East Pakistan. When the external factor (India) became decisive following the open revolt declared by Skeikh Mujibur Rahman in December 1970. Despite being the victor in the poll in terms of seats in Parliament, Mujibur Rahman was denied the Premiership. Bhutto, who hailed from West Pakistan, didn't compromise on the issue thus provoking Mujibur to declared independence.

The last element of the state is government. What type of government and how the people feel about the regime thrust upon them or made by them. If the rulers are more feared than respected, and if the power that be imposes its own language, culture, ideology and polity, then the chances of violent break up of a regime or even a country are always bright. Authoritarian regimes are vulnerable to opposition either triggered by political opponents or by a sense of injustices done against various communities and regions. So in democracy, periodic elections work as a healer when the voters get opportunity to change rulers even if such momentary decision may not necessarily be there for a long time for redressing their difficulties. Nevertheless, democratic governance is also increasingly becoming volatile due to the pulls and pressures within the ruling and opposition parties. Coalition governments in South Asia are thus becoming more ineffective in implementing policies and programs promised by the parties during elections. As it will be discussed separately in the paper, democracy's own legitimacy is likely to be on trial in coming days and years in South Asia.

II

South Asian Nations

Stories of nation-state building in South Asia would be incomplete without a short profile of each country of the region. Putting in alphabetical order, Afghanistan, a new member of the South Asian Association of Regional Cooperation (SAARC), is one of the oldest in the grouping.

Afghanistan

Afghanistan has worked as a transit to the rest of South Asia. It was therefore strategically "important location throughout the history" .Aryans, Buddhists, Zoroastrian, Islam all have mingled in Afghanistan. The Arab invasions and later its exposures to the West also influenced the culture of Afghanistan. The diversity of the country can be seen by the composition of diverse people --Pashtuns, Tajiks, Hazars, Uzbeks, Turkmen and Baloch , although Pashtuns form the largest group.

Afghanistan has still been passing through political instability since the end of monarchy in 1973. King's own relative Mohammad Sardar Daoud Khan seized power on the pretext of corruption and wretched economic conditions but failed to change the situation setting the trend of a series of coups initiated by the disgruntled Afghans with the backing of the Soviet Union. The Cold War politics thus came to the doorstep of South Asia with the Soviet Union (then superpower) and the Western powers fighting in Afghanistan. In the meantime, the rise of religious fundamentalist group (Taliban) took over power for years unless the United States took the lead to dismantle the Taliban regime through armed intervention. Today, although an elected government is holding the seat of power with the support (both military and economic) of US and other powers, there is no sign of termination of war. It thus continues to be a war-torn country. Afghanistan human development index is one the lowest in the world and in terms of global ranking , Afghanistan (174th) is ahead of only four countries, Burkina Faso, Mali, Sierra Leone and Niger, all of them in Sub-saharan Africa". Afghanistan is also the worst country from poverty index point of view.

Bangladesh

Bangladesh was part of India until partition. Its own ups and down started while it remained a part of Pakistan. Since the Muslim was/ is the dominant population of the area, it was carved out as the Eastern Wing of Pakistan. Yet, the Bengali culture and language is as integral to it as to West Bengal (India). Language issue and other disparity gaps between the West and East Pakistan plus the politics of denial were principally responsible for Bengali nationalism. And India did a part to create Bangladesh after its attempts failed to persuade the Pakistani rulers to take back ten million Bengali refugees living in India. These refugees had fled their country after the Pakistani military crack down in 1971.

It is said that there has been a "rapid" decline in depth and severity of poverty in Bangladesh. Both government and non-government sectors have contributed to this Endeavour. However, "the magnitude of poverty incidence in Bangladesh is still high—25 percent and 40 percent respectively under lower and upper poverty line". Now this figure might have been reduced, although income inequality continues to remain high in the country[4]. Political crises that often distract the direction of the country have however not allowed the country to be perennially ruled by military dictatorship.

Bhutan

The Kingdom of Bhutan is landlocked and has 7, 26000 population (2010) with more than 3 percent annual increase. The population is composed of the Drukpa, the Sharchok, and the Nepalese (Lhotsampa). Bhutan's policy of controlling immigration was initiated in 1958 and subsequently in the 1980s; its citizenship regulation became controversial when the Nepalis who had been settling there for a long time disapproved the Bhutanese strategy of denying equal rights to the Nepalese. As a result, Nepalis started moving out of the country hoping to put pressure on the Bhutanese government to retract from its citizenship policy. Some dissidents were arrested, while many leaders and innocent Bhutanese Nepalese fled the country making Nepal their first destination. About 30 thousands also settled in North Bengal, India. Such a development took place when Nepal had just restored the multiparty system in 1990 and a new elected government had taken over the charge. In the beginning, a few hundred Bhutanese entered into Nepal but the numbers swelled crossing over one hundred thousand Bhutanese in Nepal. Taking them as refugees, the United Nations took charge of maintaining them in some make-shift camps in Jhapa and Morang districts.

From the very beginning, the Nepali governments and parties mishandled the Bhutanese refugee issue and went on denouncing the Bhutanese royal regime for resorting to draconian measures to flush out the Nepalese Bhutanese. Their initial welcome to the migrants (later termed as refugees) encouraged others to leave their country with the hope that they will soon return to Bhutan with honor. But such hope proved wrong with the Bhutanese government not moving an inch towards finding a satisfactory solution to the problem. Nepal's callous approach and International sympathy to Bhutan along with India's neutrality on the issue made the Bhutanese regime inflexible. Meanwhile, US and some European countries showed their willingness to take those Bhutanese

---

4 *SAARC Regional Poverty Profile 2007*-08 (Kathmandu: SAARC Secretariat, April 2010),p.5

living in the camps to their countries. As of now, about ¾ percent refugees have been granted asylum and the remaining few are waiting for either settlement in Nepal or in the US and Europe. The government claims that a large number of the Lhotshampas are illegal immigrants who threaten the cohesion of traditional Bhutanese society, while the Lhotshampas argue that they are rightful citizens.

Bhutan is a small landlocked country having strategic significance to India. Moreover, this country is still free from political divisiveness and traumatic transition to democracy as Nepal is undergoing. Its economic growth which they call index of human happiness is noteworthy in South Asia. Its per capita income is better than those of many other South Asian countries. Its restrained policy towards tourism has enabled it to protect Bhutan's natural environment.

The traditional monarchy that came into existence in 1907 has provided stability. It has been possible due to low level of political consciousness, limited outside contacts and absorption of limited educated people in various government and non-government sectors. Some Bhutanese Nepali intelligentsia becomes a part of the bureaucracy and those who started demanding political reforms had to quit the country. And it seems that there is dim prospect of transformation of the traditional regime despite some cosmetic reforms introduced in the system a few years back. Nepal's poor performance of political parties towards institutionalizing democracy and bringing prosperity to the people might have provided a clue to the Bhutanese. Yet, in today's world, no one can predict any change, because even a minor incident or initiation may trigger off movements as have happened in Arab World or in any authoritarian regimes across the world.

India

India, like China, is also a civilization country. It is however different from China. China is homogeneous country with 92 percent Han population, while India is traditionally heterogeneous with multiple languages, cultures, religions and regions embedded with various kinds of diversities. How India has been managing its diversities and extreme forms of regionalism has become a puzzle. Now India is trying to catch China in economic development in spite of having many odds against its march to greatness. India has both political stability and economic development which in itself is worth emulating for rest of the world.

Among the South Asian countries, India's record of population growth is modest (1.38 percent) as compared to Pakistan (2.05 percent. Afghanistan, a Muslim country, has 2 percent growth rate, which can be called modest in comparison with the Maldives (2.35 percent). Sri Lanka and Bangladesh are much better with 0.74 percent and 1.76 percent respectively. The SAARC Regional Poverty Profile states that "despite significant decline in population growth rate, it is still higher than many other regions of the world; in fact lower only from SSA (Sub-Saharan Africa)"[5].

India is called a "Unnatural nation" by historian Ram Chandra Guha[6]. Reproducing Strachey's opinion, Guha writes:

> In Strachey's view, the differences between the countries of Europe were much smaller than those between the 'countries 'of India. Scotland is more like Spain than Bengal is like the Punjab'. In India the diversities of race, language and religion were far greater. Unlike in Europe, these 'countries' were not nations; they did not have distinct political or social identity. This, Strachey told his Cambridge audience, 'is the first and most essential thing to learn about India--- that there is not , and never was an India, or even any country of India possessing , according to any European ideas, any sort of unity, physical , political, social or religious"[7].

Strachey was not alone in raising the huge Indian diversities and uniqueness, many other Western scholars were also skeptical about the Indian state's capacity to maintain its unity. Guha also says that "there was no Indian nation or country in the past; nor would there be one in the future"[8].

India is one of the most difficult nations to govern because of its size, diversity, democracy and inherited caste and class hierarchies. As Zoya Hasan has rightly pointed out about the Indian situation in these words:

> India is undeniably one of the world's most unequal societies.

---

5 Ibid.,p.11

6 See Ram Chandra Guha, *India After Gandhi: The History of the* World's *Largest Democracy* (London: Macmillan, 2007),p.xi

7 John Strachey, *India* (London: Kegan, Paul, 1888), pp.2-5. See Guha, Ibid,p. xiii.

8 Ibid.

Social inequality revolves around the axes of class, caste, tribal status, religion, and gender. Inter-group disparities are sharply marked, with major contrasts of social conditions and chances of sharing in society's material and cultural resources--- that is, income, employment, education, health, and so on. These inequalities are rooted in the caste system, property, income, wealth, and employment relations. The upper castes are the most advantaged in India and the Scheduled Castes (SCs) and Scheduled Tribes (STs) among the poorest and most disadvantaged...Low caste status is often accompanied by deprivation, and traditional and historical forms of social inequality thus coexist with, and , are reinforced by, inequalities arising out of the sphere of production and economic activity[9] .

Yet, while presenting such a picture of India, Its positive aspects are also simultaneously highlighted by scholars taking India as one of the exciting countries insofar as social and political engineering is concerned. Hasan herself has admitted it by writing that "India is one of the few countries in the post-colonial world that took up the challenge of building an inclusive democracy in a highly diverse, multicultural, multilingual, and multi-religious society"[10].

India became a unified nation- state after independence. Yet, its larger entity in the pre-1947 period had given it the status of a country. All former princely states were integrated soon after independence making the new independent centralized union of states. The constitution promulgated on January 26, 1950 called the new entity as union of states as the United States preferred to give the name of United States because of the original thirteen members whose number has now gone up to 50. Indian's federal system has different characteristics – 'cooperative', 'bargaining' and 'centralized'. In fact, cooperation is the basis of any kind of federal structure. No conflict situation promotes the spirit of federalism. Even if some conflicts arise between federating units, they need to be tackled by the mechanism developed by the constitution. And centre plays a part in mitigating grievances of various states. Bargaining federalism highlights the demand side of states (provinces) that put pressures on the Centre to

---

9 Zoya Hasan, *Politics of Inclusion: Castes, Minorities and Affirmative Action* (New DelhI: Oxford University Press, 2009), p.3.

10 Ibid. See also Atul Kohli ed., *The Success of India's Democracy (Cambridge: Cambridge University Press, 2001).*

address their grievances by allocating resources etc. However, all such bargaining deals would have to be managed by cooperation of the actors involved. Centralized federalism was at its peak until the opposition parties came to power in various states. Governments were dismissed by the centre on various pretexts. Now cooperative element is more pronounced than centrally directed state.

India has huge population of more than one billion which, if the present trend continues, may over take China by 2020. India's population size, social diversities, poverty and crises of governance have often given rise to despondency. The neo-liberal economy that has accelerated the rate of growth has not yet covered the sizable section of poverty stricken population.

Indian paranoia and a sense of vulnerability can be observed in the psychology of elites. A small incident or deaths of Prime Ministers or famine or centrifugal tendencies faced by the country or declining influence of national parties and its negative repercussions on the stability of democracy and governments make Indians disturbed. Sometimes, the fear of military take over is also raised, though Indian army is still considered to be fully under control of civilian government. Military take over as of now seems to be a distant possibility in India and Sri Lanka or even in Nepal because of each country's own historical and political context.

The Maldives

The Maldives consist of 26 natural atolls, comprising 1,192 islands and has very little physical territory. Even a visitor to the capital, Male, has to use the boat as if the boat all over the Maldives is only a mode of transport. Maldives has a small population of 300,000, mostly Muslim. Southern India and Sri Lanka have influenced in shaping the ethnic composition of the Republic. The people are ethnically known as Dhivehis. Maldives's source of income is fishing and tourism which is increasingly becoming attractive for those who want to spend a few days in serene place and seclusion. This unique place had experienced the Portuguese, Dutch and British rule and got independence in 1965 from the last British colonial rule. Maumoon Abdul Gayoom ruled this sea-locked country for twenty nine years until his authoritarian regime was toppled in 2008 by the combined force of people. In 2009, democratic elections were held for parliament and President with the hope of ushering in new era of democratic stability and development. However, the elected President was charged with illegal ordering of arrest of a judge provoking his opponents to go against him. The army and the former pro-Gayoom elements joined together to oust President Nasheed and also to put Vice President, Mohammad Waheed Hassan, as the new president of the republic. India and other external powers later supported the new government. Such uncertain politics cannot enhance the prospect of nation state building.

Nepal

Nepal is a landlocked country sharing borders with China and India, the two emerging powers of the world. Nepal's total population as of 2011 census is 26 million. Nepal's ethnic mosaic and harmony were considered as exemplary in the world because of the coming ling of different socio-cultural and religious moorings. However, with the rise of political awareness of people, ethnic communities, caste and regional groups are now demanding due share in state structures to which people unaccustomed to such instant stirs tend to see these trends as hastening the process of disintegration of the country. Nepal, like India, is predominantly a Hindu state (81 percent) followed by the Buddhists (5 percent, Muslim and others 5 percent). Historically, Nepal became a single territorial entity after the Shah conquest, called unification, in 1769 and later with the expansion of territories in the East and West. Small principalities and kingdoms were integrated either by conquest or by design forged by the Kings. Nepal is an independent country throughout its modern history. Its syncretic culture and moderate religious tradition could provide it with a distinct national identity.

The past tradition however is being revisited in order to strike a balance between the past and present. For, both 'primordialists' and 'instrumentalists' have stuck their positions in the post-2006 *Jan andolan* (mass movement). According to Edward Shils and Clifford Geetz, the primordialists are those who continue to embrace religion, blood relations, language, custom etc., while the instrumentalists try to use ethnicity as social, political, cultural resource for different interest-status groups[11]. For the first time in Nepali history, such ethnic and regional upsurge has been witnessed in the post-2006 movement with all the sections of society

11 As mentioned in John Hutchison & Anthony D. Smith, eds., Ethnicty (oxford: Oxford University Press, 1996),p.8.

advancing their own agendas of power sharing and identity. They argue that the old policy of national integration and assimilation imposed on them by the centralized state cannot ensure the much touted agenda of 'inclusiveness' and empowerment of all people belonging to a defined territory[12]

Single identity-based   vs. plural identity based federal units debate has generated enough heat to which no political parties have shown any clue to reconciling such differences. And parties' leaders and stakeholders can only resolve it by entering into a series of negotiations before they finalize the draft of the new constitution. It has been debated that the issue of restructuring of state along ethnic/non-ethnic line was the principal reason for the failure of political parties to make a constitution by the dissolved CA. However it is crystal clear that without addressing the issue of federalism with utmost sense of flexibility, no constitution can be enforced in Nepal.

Nation building is as much a political agenda as it is an economic agenda. Economically, Nepal was/ is an   adjunct to the Indian economy. Economic dependence on India was evident after the British Raj established its sway in India. So only nominal trade connection remained with Tibet until the latter became People's Autonomous Region of China. Nepal's policy of diversification of economic relations was pursued after the 1960 Royal coup with Nepal opening up market to 'foreign goods" imported from third countries i.e. beyond India. Chinese and other countries' goods not only flooded the Nepali market but they also allegedly found way to crazy Indian consumers. However, it did not help develop Nepal's economic infrastructure as unscrupulous traders in connivance with politicians, bureaucrats and security agencies helped foster such illegal trade which neither helped Nepal nor India. Only a novo riche or what is called in Nepali a Bhuin *Phutta Barga*, was created through the get rich quick psychology. Capital formation that could be used for economic development which eventually leads to employment generation and distributive justice was not possible due to such unholy alliance between foreign goods agents and the various structures of government.

Thus, Nepal's economic backwardness can be attributed to bad politics which is characterized by lack of political vision of core political

---

12 For a full account of various dimensions of state building, see Krishna Hachhethu, *State Building in Nepal: creating a Functional State* (Kathmandu: ESP,2009).

leaders, chair-centric priority of parties' leaders, lack of national consensus for developing minimum common program of overall development of the country, political instability and conflict in political culture,. Nepal's huge water resource (actual achievable capacity of 43,000 Mw) remains unutilized plunging the country into darkness and depending on the monsoon rain for cultivation. Similarly, Nepal continues to be plagued by the permanent trade deficit to the extent that the government controlled Nepal Oil Corporation cannot pay dues to Indian Oil Corporation prompting the latter to stop fuel supply in every now and then. Other indicators such as education, public sector enterprises, and others also suggest that Nepal's international credibility is all time low. Crises of governance and lack of political direction can be singled out as the most important negative factors for obstructing the task of nation building.

Pakistan

Pakistan's traumatic history of nation building begins with the very morrow of the birth of the country in 1947. The death of the father of the nation, Jinnah, and assassination of his successor, Liaquat Ali Khan in 1951, lost the direction of institutionalization and development paving the way for a series of political instability prodding the military generals to stage coups from time to time. Even while the so-called elected governments were in place, the army continued to keep its veto power. Sometimes, the military and sometimes the judiciary seem to determine the fate of governments. Recently, the Supreme Court has forced the elected Prime Minister, Yousaf Raza Gilani, to quit office on the grounds of the contempt of court. Gilani was asked to reopen the case of corruption against President Asif Ali Zardari suspecting that the latter has stacked money in the Swiss Bank. Gilani refused to write such a letter in order to furnish information on the President's account because the President has certain immunities according to Constitution and hence cannot be moved any case against him so long as he remains a president. The same situation is being repeated in the case of Gilani's successor as the Court has once again given the new Prime Minister to write a letter within July 25, 2010 [extended to August 8] failing of which would mean contempt of court. In this context, a Pakistani scholar, Wasim, has written in detail in his latest article " Judging democracy in Pakistan: Conflict between the executive and judiciary". He writes:

We can conclude that the courts' operations in an activist mode has the potential to discredit a civilian government that operates within the framework of a military dominated power structure, with scant resources at its disposal to survive in office for long or to safeguard the system from breakdown. At the same time, the Supreme Court remained wedded to the idea of restraint by talking about the high principles of accountability and demands of justice in the court proceedings, but gave final judgments based on a balancing act, letting the government off the hook in critical moments and withdrawing at the point at which it would have undermined the prevalent setup. The Court's behavior approximated the pattern of a modus Vivendi as practised in India rather than an exercise in straight-jacketing the incumbent government altogether. (Mehta 2006, 172–3) In a final sense, the judiciary in Pakistan re-established the legal idiom as an overarching framework for politics[13].

Pakistan is one of the most unfortunate countries in South Asia. Its trauma of political development and nation building is perennial. Today the country is plagued by continued social, regional and class disparities, religious fundamentalism, terrorism and foreign interventions besides being politically volatile and uncertain. Minorities within the broad Muslim communities are at war with the state. The Baluchistan and Sind are ravaged by conflicts. As Urmila Phadnis states," The goals of the Baluch national movement range from autonomy, confederation, secession to irredentism"[14]. Now in other parts of Pakistan also, violence has become a regular phenomenon. Languages, religion, intense feelings of disparity continue to spark violence. The Mohajirs in Sind, who migrated from Gujarat, Bombay and other parts of India want to preserve their identity. One million Ahamadi population in Pakistan are declared illegal "to act or look like Muslim, to practice or propagate their faith and to call their worship place a mosque". The Shiites feel insecure vis a vis the Sunnis of Pakistan. Other Muslims also inherit their animosities with the dominant communities. Such multiple areas of conflict are thus rooted not only in politics but also in social, economic, regional and religious fields making Pakistan a country under permanent seizes.

---

13 Mohammad Wasim, "Judging democracy in Pakistan: Conflict Between the executive and judiciary", *Contemporary South Asia* (Lahore), 20:1: 2012, pp.19-31.

14 See Urmila Phadnis, *Ethnicity and* Nation *Building in South Asia* (New Delhi: Sage publications, 1990), p.175.

Sri Lanka

Sri Lanka is an island nation with 20.5 million people and traumatic social and political contexts. Sinhalese (74 percent) are the dominant group followed by the Tamil (indigenous 12.7 percent) and Indian immigrants (5.5. percent). The latter category came to Ceylon (now Sri Lanka) as tea plantation workers during the British Raj. Sri Lanka's modern historical links with the British were responsible for making it a liberal democracy country after independence in 1948. The Sinhala- Tamil animosity developed after the Sinhala dominated governments failed to assuage the feelings of deprivation of Tamil minority. Since i983, the indigenous Sri Lankan declared war against the political order dominated by the Sinhalese. It came to an end only a few years ago following the full scale war declared by President Mahinda Rajapaksha, who is "widely credited as being a key architect of that military victory and has moved to consolidate his popularity and hold on power on this basis"[15]. President Rajapaksha has made a pledge recently that he would try to pursue the agenda of rehabilitation of the displaced Tamils.

III

Challenges and Prospects

The theoretical underpinnings of nation building would be lopsided if both the terms are not made as an organic whole. For, states, in fact, are also the nations, as stated before; its elements can be coterminous with the strategies of nation building which is basically people-centric if we also take it in totality irrespective of caste, creed, and ethnicity and so on. From this perspective, most countries of South Asia lack many ingredients among which institutionalized political order, inclusive/ participatory democracy, universally established democratic culture and popular sovereignty , social justice, secular state, casteless, if not classless societies and states. What other developed states had settled some of these elements centuries ago, many South Asian states are besieged now by similar conflicts. Secularism, for instance, continues to be a controversial aspect for defining and regulating a modern South Asian state. Only India has established its tradition even while being a predominantly Hindu state.

---

15 Paikiasothy saravanamuttu, " The Presidency and Conflict Resolution: The Case of Sri Lanka" in Lok Raj Baral ed., *Constitutional Government and Democracy in South Asia* (Kathmandu: Nepal centre for contemporary studies, 2011),p.145

Concern shown to the minorities and other deprived sections of society is not ritualistic in India despite grievances raised by various minority communities.

The Bharatiya Janata Party (BJP) in India was originated as Jana Sangh that championed the cause of Hindus, but now it has modified its previous position realizing the changed political context against which no national party could garner support for winning elections. Nevertheless, the BJP has been maligned as a non-secular party by its so-called secular detractors and has often blocked its way to power. However, this party has come to power when its principal adversary, the Congress, failed to win. It is also interesting to note that both the national parties are on the decline in recent years and their prospects of power depend on their capacity to build coalition with other regional parties.

Bangladesh followed the Indian pattern after achieving independence in 1971 with Sheikh Mujibur Rahman declaring four underlined principles of the Provisional Constitution of Bangladesh Order, 1972. These principles were: Socialism, secularism, democracy and nationalism. The constitution of the Kingdom of Nepal, 1959 was silent on the issue of religion though it mentioned the sovereign (the King) as Hindu. Secularism has now been adopted as one of the tenets of Republican Nepal contrary to the opinion of a tiny section of population to hold referendum on determining Hindu state or secular state. Some traditional Hindu monarchists want to make it a political issue setting foothold on the terrain of secularism and republican system.

The politics of regionalism and ethnicity has added new dimensions in the politics of the region. It has both positive and negative effects on nation-state project of South Asia. Regional parties in India which were perceived in the beginning as representing the trends of fragmentation of politics and nation are now considered as the embodiment of true spirit of nation building. These parties blow up their regional issues in order to maximize favour of the Centre but they too play the role of proving stability to the polity. Indian situation is being replicated in Nepal with ethnic, region and other agendas of identity politics looming large in the nation building endeavors. The rise of Tarai (Madhesh) parties, ethnic and dalit groups (plus others) have forced the so-called big parties to set such agendas that suit the cause of them. Its immediate implications were seen in the composition of the Constituent Assembly (CA) in 2008. In the dissolved CA all these groups could swell their numbers (representation) compared to the three parliamentary elections held in 1991, 1994 and 1999. Only marginally, these groups were represented in both the Houses of Parliament[16].

Bangladesh's pattern of representation has considerably improved in recent years. Minority rights, migrant workers' rights, women rights have become important aspects of Civil Society movements. Yet, some minority groups such as Hindus and Buddhists (Chakras) still feel insecure in face of rising trends of Islamic fundamentalism. Since Bangladesh politics is basically "street-centric" rather than parliament-centric because of the lack of healthy opposition within parliament, the two major parties--- the National Awami League and Bangladesh Nationalist Parties' ---do not see eye to eye as opposition leaders in India, Nepal and even Pakistan do. Amena Moshin states that "boycott of the parliament by the opposition is the norm rather than exception irrespective of the party"[17].

Negative party politics that breed contempt, distrust, corruption, governmental inefficiency, economic stagnation and incredible situation in international relations has great impacts on the life of a nation. Some are relatively better than others and therefore cannot be put in the same basket. Countries like Afghanistan and Nepal are plagued by such trends, while Bangladesh and Sri Lanka are much better than them, and Pakistan continues to be unpredictable due to signs of instability. Politically, Nepal is embroiled in many of the above mentioned trends, but remains a dynamic country in social change and religious proselytization. No religious fanaticism seems to loom large even when the country is passing through a turbulent phase in its modern history. Yet, politically, Nepal continues to be a 'nation-state in the wilderness' as I have discussed under the same title in a book published in 2012.

The Class structure of South Asia remains the same with the middle or upper-middle class people dominating the entire activities of the countries of the region. India has made economic strides in recent years, but the magnitude of poverty, rampant corruption eating the vitals of polity, and fragmentary nature of coalition politics, leadership role and

16 See the Results of CA election, 2008.

17 Amena Mohsin, "Bangladesh Parliament: Trapped in Politics of Confrontation", in Lok Raj Baral, ed., *Constitutional Government And Democracy in South Asia* (Kathmandu: Nepal Centre for Contemporary Studies, 2001),p.74

organizational deficiency have made the system weak to upgrade the level of development.

Generally, during the nationalist and democratic movements in South Asia, all ethnic and other groups were mobilized behind a single agenda of self-rule. Now ethnic movements have taken space in national politics forcing political elites to be responsible and inclusive. Paul Brass has said,

> ...” it is not inequality as such or relative deprivation or status discrepancies that are the critical precipitants of nationalism in ethnic groups, but the relative distribution of ethnic groups in the competition for valued resources and opportunities and in the division of labour in societies undergoing social mobilization, industrialization, and bureaucratization. The potential for ethnic nationalism exists when there is a system of ethnic stratification in which one ethnic group is dominant over another, but it is not usually realized until some members form one ethnic groups attempt to move into the economic niches occupied by the rival ethnic groups “[18].

Now terrorism of various kinds and intensity has entered into the lives of nation states in South Asia. Internally, many countries are in perpetual wars against some kinds of terrorism (national and international), and insurgencies waged for both regime change and independence or identity. Poor countries' capacity to counter terrorism is not adequate. So they are under intense pressure to invite foreign intervention, which, in turn, becomes contentious within the country. The NATO and US forces in Afghanistan need to use Pakistan as a corridor for supplies of goods and weapons provoking the Taliban guerrillas to retaliate with maximum force. It has threatened Pakistan's security as well.

Some states have managed to contain internal terrorism by using state power or by making compromises for new autonomous regions. Countries under intense ethnic and regional pressures seem to be in dilemma as to how far they can accommodate such pressures. Internal insurgencies that are also taken as 'terrorist groups' have invariably failed to achieve their objectives without making compromises with the state. Yet, they cannot be totally ignored by the state because of their own attractive agendas and demands concerning the down trodden people.

---

18 Paul R. Brass, *Ethnicity and nationalism:* Thoery *and comparison (New DelhI: sage publication, 1991), p.47.*

Nepal is one of the countries of the region where different social groups have put up demands before the major parties that they should be treated equally as any other dominant caste or class groups. It has been said that the caucus created by members of the CA (now dissolved) has embarrassed their parties' bosses who have rejected the demand of creating autonomous provinces based on ethnicity. Alarmed at the demand of ethnic-based federalism, the high caste groups (Bahun-Chhetri) with more than 30 percent population have also demanded that they be recognized as ethnic categories. These groups are especially annoyed with the political parties that put them in the Interim Constitution (2007) as *anya (*others*)*. The tug of war is on regarding the ethnic-based federalism or federalism based on plural identities.

However, federalism cannot be devised without taking into account the identity politics based on ethnicity and resources and capacity of each province to be created by the constitution. Many people, who have not experienced similar situation through the modern Nepali history because of the centralized unitary state structure in the past, think that sudden upsurge of ethnic and regional demands and divisions created by them in the country would pave the way for its own disintegration. But, given the nature and background of Nepali society, it is not as much alarming as is made out by the anti-federalist groups. It may produce ripples for the time being, but once the major forces and stake holders sit together for arriving at a solution, it is likely to be settled.

Conclusion

Conventional political wisdom and practices have undergone a sea-change in South Asia. The state-centered approach is being re-examined for making nation-state more inclusive and accommodative. Some countries are trying to continue the parliamentary system with reforms so as to adjust it to the changed context of multiparty politics. Now the two party system is no more the ideal model of parliamentary system as multi-parties based on regionalism and ethnicity etc. have in fact dominated the politics both at the Center and local levels. So political ideology as a principle has been relegated to the subordinate position, though the framework of liberal democracy is evoked by all the parties ---Left, Right and Centrist, regional and ethnic. Conceivably, nationalism as was understood against the context of foreign rule and native traditional authoritarianism, has ceased to be a unifying factor if it fails to pursue a policy of inclusiveness and empowerment of various social groups irrespective of castes, class, ethnicity, region and gender. Demands for inclusiveness and empowerment have also widened the arenas of nation building. High rate of economic growth with a bias for alleviation of poverty, end of social disparity by pursuing aggressive policies of the state and other private sectors, capacity to choose appropriate ideology and approaches to national reconstruction in all its ramifications, and attitudinal change on the part of elites and effective leadership role can enlarge the scope of nation building. Since many of them are lacking in South Asia, peoples are increasingly becoming impatient with the established regimes and elites.

One of the important aspects of nation building is strong executive (legitimate). South Asian governments that come from a variety of social-economic and political backgrounds are bereft of such strong and stable leadership that can push the people-centric socio-economic agendas. Thus far, there are no discernible trends of elite transformation in South Asian political context. So the same categories of rulers alternate their turn, despite some changes witnessed in elections in recent years. Political power either at the centre or in provinces and districts continues to be the exclusive domain of middle and upper middle class people. Nevertheless, a new popular upsurge is witnessed in South Asia for making democracy more humane and vibrant. The common people also know that their actual power will not be realized unless they are fully empowered socially, economically and politically.

Secular values are the hallmarks of modern nation state. South Asia is partly secular in that most countries either naturally inherit the tradition of social harmony or are secular by design. India is secular both by design and traditions despite occasional resurfacing of communal violence. It is however gratifying to note that incidence of communal or sectarian violence in India is less compared to its past records. Only grievances of minorities and oppressed and suppressed sections get focused in political discourses and media.

Pakistan is still reeled under sectarian and regional conflicts or has even been harassed by the new wave of terrorism, both externally induced and internally originated. Sri Lanka too is conflict-prone even after having ended the twenty five year -long ethnic war. It is under pressure to become a conflict-free country by devising various policy measures to assuage minorities' feelings of insecurity and deprivation.

South Asia is basically a conflict-torn region. All countries have asymmetrical level of development in terms of size, population, and political stability. Paralysis seems to creep in the management of political order in the region's countries. Political leaders are under seize because of their incapacity to govern, to reduce poverty and to harmonize conflicting interests of haves and haves not. As a result, peoples are loosing faith in the political orders adopted by the countries of the region. . A new disequilibrium has thus emerged with the multiplying crises. They have made democracy weak and irrelevant to mitigating the problems of people. It does not however mean that the South Asian nations are breaking up as had been prophesized about India by some Western scholars in the 1960s. For, South Asian nation states have many positive aspects that do not portend immediate trends of disintegration. Defying all prophesies of doom, language, culture and common and civilizational linkages, flexibility displayed by leadership, though   paradoxical, continue to hold them together.

India's Federalism And The Practice of Politics: Challenges And Possibilities[1]

Bishnu N. Mohapatra

On 26 November 2008 - terror struck Mumbai, a horrific event that scarred several lives in the city forever. Nearly 190 people killed and more than 350 injured, the city experienced a new kind of vulnerability that it has not encountered before. It is not that violence was new to Mumbai, nor was it the first terrorists attack in the city. What was new, however, was the nature of the attack, and the fact that lurking behind the tragedy was a network of people, organization, intelligence and resources that was simultaneously local, national and global. As this tragedy slowly gets deposited on the existing pile of city's dreadful memories, the governments – both the federal and the state – struggle to strengthen the existing institutions and create new ones to fight against any future acts of terror.

For a while the government of India is trying to create a National Counter Terrorism Centre (NCTC), a federal body whose outreach can extend to state governments' jurisdiction. According to the proposed plan, NCTC has the power of interrogation, seizure, and arrest in any part of the country under the Unlawful Activities (Prevention) Act. Several state governments – predictably the non-Congress ones- expressed their reservations against the establishment of NCTC in its proposed incarnation. Federal anti-terror laws (TADA- Terrorist and Disruptive Activities Prevention Act and POTA – Prevention of Terrorism Act) in the past had evoked strong reactions from different organizations including the State Governments and human rights networks. The critique largely rested on the laws' possible excesses, misuses and their potential for undermining human rights of citizens. However, this time round, NCTC is critiqued for its anti-federal impulse. Narendra Modi- the Chief Minister of Gujarat – accused the Centre for changing the "well-defined

---

1 (South Asia: Nation Building and Federalism, a regional conference organized by Nepal Centre for Contemporary Studies, Kathmandu, Dhulikhel Lodge Resort, Nepal, August 26 &27 2012)

and constitutionally mandated" boundaries of Centre-state relations. He provocatively remarked that the Centre "(is) behaving like the viceroys of the yore".[2] Chief Ministers belonging to seven states such as Uttar Pradesh, West Bengal, Tamil Nadu, Chhattisgarh, Odisha, Punjab, and Jammu and Kashmir also fear that NCTC would interfere in the states' rights in the matters of law and order. In the meeting of the Chief Ministers convened by the Home Minister of the government of India to discuss NCTC in May 2012, the opponents argued that the 'autocratic' attitude of the Centre 'militated against all cannons of federalism'[3]. It is now clear that for NCTC to be established, the government of India not merely needs to allay the fears of the state governments but also has to change its style of engagement with them.

Federalism after all is not merely about substance of power but also about a political style, an engagement and a way of aligning different domains of governance. It is against the touchstone of practices (not merely the intent) that India's federalism has to be understood and judged. This paper is an attempt to do it. Looking at federal practices for the last sixty-two years one can argue that on the whole they have succeeded in balancing the imperatives of national unity with the claims of regional and linguistic diversities in India. But this is a larger, macro-level story. Like all macro-level stories, it can gloss over many micro dimensions and ground-level experiences. For instance, if one looks at the North-East and Jammu and Kashmir, the federal story appears very different. One can argue that wherever and whenever the establishment of order and writ of the Indian nation-state become the prime mover and determinant of things, federal practices get attenuated. Aspirations for autonomy –within the boundary of India- particularly in these areas suffer major setbacks. However, the established, politically mobilized and territorially embedded linguistic / cultural groups have fared well within the Indian federal polity. But smaller language groups and minorities including the tribal communities are not sufficiently empowered by the existing vision of federalism. While summing up India's federal practices, one has to take into account the particularities of the experiences of the groups /communities at the margins.

2　*The Hindu*, May 5 2012

3　*The Hindu* May 5 2012

This takes me to the final argument. From the vantage point of decentralization /democratization, India's federalism has a long way to go. The values of sharing of power and that of devolution have not been adequately stitched as yet. Although through the 73rd and 74th amendments of 1992, the project of decentralization has been constitutionalized in India, the federal vision and practice continue to be trapped within a dyadic framework. The state governments wish to snatch more power from the Centre, but they are not necessarily willing to devolve them to local governments. If the Centre can be hegemonic, so can be the states.

The local self-government is yet to emerge as a respectable domain of politics in India. The point of arguing this is not to undermine the achievement of India's federal experiment. Undoubtedly, it has given Indian politics and governance its accommodating thrust. However, the federal logic is constantly evolving, and much of the evolution is shaped by its strength and also by its contradictions. There are four elements of the present conjuncture that influence the federal governance in India: the ongoing process of economic liberalization, the emergence of coalition politics at the Centre and the regionalization of politics and finally the continuing presence of exclusivist nationalism. Together, they push India's federalism in different directions not anticipated fully by the architects of the constitution.

I

It would be anachronistic to suggest that federal norms were always a part of India's governance architecture in the past. Indian federalism that we discuss here is intimately connected to modern state-forms and geographies of power. However if one were to look through the long tunnel of history one could see that the ancient 'Indian' empires had devised innovative ways of engaging with and managing regional kingdoms and communities based on geographical, linguistic, cultural and religious diversities. Whether the state-form of those empires was monolithic or segmentary is not the issue here. Division of empire into sub-units, allowing regional kingdoms to exercise their authority within their territories, distribution and diffusion of symbolic power were some of the strategies by which larger political systems were sustained. It is not surprising that some scholars suggest that the earlier state-form embodying a dialectical relationship with the sub-continental empire finds its modern manifestation in the Indian federal forms[4].

However, the evolution of federalism in its modern incarnation can be traced to the British colonial period. The Indian provinces under the British rule were a product of annexation and arbitrary divisions. Large presidencies such as Bengal and Madras were composed of huge number of distinct communities and regions. But with the passage of time, administrative and pragmatic reasons prompted the British not only to initiate institutional reforms but also to offer limited representation to the educated/ propertied Indian classes.

This is not the place to do a detailed narrative of all the key administrative reforms initiated by the colonial state in India. It is worthwhile to suggest that although in the late nineteenth century the Indian Councils Act of 1861 inaugurated some division of power between the central authority and the local legislature, the Government of India Acts of 1909 and 1919 created a modicum of provincial power with some responsibilities but with strong oversight and control. The Government of India Act of 1919 that followed the Montagu-Chelmsford Reforms institutionalized more power for the provincial legislature and a division of power between it and the Central government. The 1935 Government of India Act was a significant turning point as far as the evolution of federalism in India was concerned. It not only established a dual system of government with clear division of power, it also created new possibilities for political mobilization at the provincial level. Except for the proposal articulated by the Cabinet Mission Plan in 1946 that provided for a relatively weak Centre and strong provincial government, most of the ideas generated within the colonial constitutional experiments were, not surprisingly, excessively 'unitary'.

If the colonial administrative/political reforms created new (albeit limited) opportunities for establishing a federal polity, the peoples' linguistic and ethnic assertions in different parts of India gave this process a new momentum and urgency. Early on Gandhi saw in these stirrings, in such restless collective energy, a new possibility for anti-colonial mobilization. It is therefore not surprising that in the Nagpur session in

---

4 Lloyd I. Rudolph and Susanne Hoeber Rudolph: "State Formation in India: Building and Wasting Assets", and also see "The Sub continental Empire and the Regional Kingdom in Indian State Formation", in their Explaining Indian Democracy: A Fifty-Year Perspective, 1956-2006, Volume II, Delhi: Oxford University Press, 2008.

1920 the linguistic reorganization of the Congress was approved. By the beginning of the twentieth century, the linguistic/ regional consciousness was growing in many parts of the colonial India. By acknowledging their aspirations, the Congress created a strong link between linguistic nationalism (sub-nationalism, little nationalism as some literature describes them) and all-India nationalism. By the 1930s India witnessed a generation of leaders in different provinces who were declaring themselves as simultaneously Indian and regional nationalists. Most of them did not see any contradiction between a strong Indian nation and a strong regional/ provincial identity. This was no mean achievement, and it is arguable that this sentiment created a strong moral /ideational foundation on which Indian federal polity would be constructed after the independence in 1947. This federal spirit in turn gave the Indian nationalism its ecumenical character, its inclusiveness and its expansive rendition.

Therefore it does not come as a surprise when Granville Austin, a renowned authority on the constitution-making process in India, suggests that the 'most singular aspect of the drafting of the federal provisions was the relative absence of conflict between the 'centralizers' and the 'provincialists'[5]. It may not be seen as an 'overlapping consensus' in a Rawlsian sense, but it was good enough a compact at the time to push an idea of a centralizing federal system firmly into the political horizon of divergent political actors engaged in the making of the constitution. There is no doubt that the partition of the British India had a startling impact on the proceedings of the Constituent Assembly that was set up following the Cabinet Mission Plan in 1946. Even though the Muslim League boycotted it, the initial recommendations of the Union Power Committees for a weak Centre and strong provincial governments were essentially to accommodate its interest. Once the partition was announced in June 1947, and the communal conflagration that followed it, it altered the context of constitution-making dramatically. Or that is what it appears from the narrative of the constituent assembly debates. The revised report submitted by the Union Power Committee argued that, "it would be injurious to the interest of the country to provide for a weak cultural authority which would be incapable of ensuring peace, of coordinating vital matters of common concern, and of

---

5   Granville Austin (1966), The Indian Constitution: Cornerstone of a Nation, Oxford: Clarendon Press, chapter -8, p. 186.

speaking effectively for the whole country in the international sphere…the soundest framework for our constitution is a federation with a strong Centre"[6]. It is the partition that shifted the discussion on minority rights, provincial autonomy and residuary power in a centralizing direction. The question of unity and integrity of a new emerging nation also came to occupy a larger space in the minds of the Congress leaders. But for all its soundness, it remains a partial explanation.

The idea of a strong Centre was evidently embedded within the colonial statecraft and governance. The Indian political leaders were quite familiar with these practices. The attraction of the familiar also pushed the debate in a centralizing direction. One of the key structural arguments provided was that it was a strong central government that could address social problems and exigencies such as providing security to people, rehabilitating refugees, combating food crisis and steering economy and development. There was also a larger consensus among the top leadership of the Congress that a strong Central government is necessary in order to govern a large and diverse India. As early as 1936, at a time when Congress was committed to the aspirations of the linguistic groups, Nehru guessed that, "it (is) likely that free India may be a federal India, though in any event there must be great deal of unitary control"[7].

The idea of 'unitary control' in some sense emerged from and connected to the imaginary of a nation-state in India. Since the nineteenth century, Indian leaders and reformers always felt that India in the past suffered largely due to the absence of a centralized nation-state. Some of them argued that the presence of strong nation-states allowed the 'west' to dominate the rest of societies in Asia and Africa. Therefore building a strong nation-state was an inevitable step in order to achieve 'modernity'. Gandhi's views on these issues were very different. But by the time India finalized the constitution, these ideas had already become the relics of the past or being interpreted as an unrealizable utopia. However, the clamour for regional identity and search for political power within the province could never be fully drowned by the narratives of Indian nationalism. This kept the federal discourse alive in realms of collective action and politics

---

6 Austin (1966), p. 190.

7 Austin (1966), p. 189.

in different parts of India.

II

India's constitutional federal democracy began its journey in 1950. The first election in 1951 put the elected national and provincial governments in place, and the National Congress' dominance provided a semblance of stability to the structure of democratic governance. Despite this, the issue of reorganization of provinces, an unfinished business from the constitution-making days, resurfaced with intensity. Regional and linguistic passions ran high. Predictably, this passion had frightened the ultra-Indian nationalists in the past. Even liberal nationalists like Nehru were not entirely convinced of its appeal and rationality. Although the Congress was committed to the reorganization of provinces on linguistic lines since the 1920s, the post-partition environment made this issue to appear in a different light. At the heart of it were two very different views about Indian nation and nationalism. Some senior leaders like Nehru, Rajendra Prasad and Abdul Kalam Azad viewed the regional assertion from a linguistic identity point of view as narrow and had the potential to undermine national civic efforts on development and welfare. On the contrary the regional nationalists saw their demand as democratic and were convinced that re-organization of provinces would not only enhance state governments' legitimacy but also foster greater national solidarity.

It is not surprising that during the constituent assembly period, the Dar Commission[8] and the JVP[9] Committee were not in support of creating new provinces on the basis of language. JVP's position was largely pragmatic rather than principled. It also believed that "if public sentiment is insistent and overwhelming, we as democrats have to submit to it, but subject to certain limitations in regard to the good of India as a whole"[10].

Soon the intensity of public sentiments forced Nehru to change his view about reorganization of provinces. The Andhra agitation opened the floodgate. Andhra Pradesh – predominantly

---

8   A commission set up in 1948 by three members led by the former judge of the Allahabad High Court S. K. Dar. The other two members were J. N. Lal and Panna Lall.

9   JVP- the acronym refers to the names of the committee members: Jawaharlal Nehru, Vallabh Bhai Patel and Pattabhi Sitaramaya. This report was submitted on 1 April 1949.

10 Austin (1966), p. 242.

Telugu-speaking areas- was constituted as a separate province in 1953, and a State Reorganization Commission was set up in 1954. Following the recommendation of the Commission in 1956, the process of reorganizing provinces began. The colonial legacy that reflected in the groupings of the states (A, B, C & D) gave way to two simple categories: provinces and union territories. The province of Bombay was divided into Maharashtra and Gujarat in an acrimonious atmosphere in 1960. In 1966, Punjab was divided into two states: Haryana and Punjab. Himachal Pradesh was carved out of Punjab in 1971. Nagaland was made into a province in 1963 as a way of bringing peace to the state. Some of the north-eastern states – Manipur, Meghalaya, Tripura and Mizoram- were elevated to statehood in 1972. Sikkim was incorporated as a state of the Indian Union in 1975. The last major reorganization of states took place in 2000 when three new states – Chhattisgarh, Jharkhand and Uttaranchal – were created out of Madhya Pradesh, Bihar and Uttar Pradesh respectively. This certainly is not the last we saw of the creation of separate provinces in India.

It is easy to see that reorganization of states on the basis of ethnicity and language has become an accepted part of India's federal discourse. It does not evoke strong reactions as it did in the 1950s. It is also true that religion-based demand for re-drawing territories is strongly jettisoned today as it was in the 1940s and 1950s. The public policy discourse even today continues to be squeamish about handling religious identity or groups' demand although special programmes for the welfare of religious minorities are enacted from time to time by the federal and several state governments in India. Insofar as the Indian constitution allows the central government to alter the boundary of the provinces, it is understandable why groups demanding separate province always appeal to the good sense of the Centre. The Centre in turn tries to create a consensus before agreeing to the demands of the protestors. The ongoing agitation for the creation of Telengana (a separate province to be carved out of Andhra Pradesh) is a striking example of this. Reflecting on the peculiarity of Indian federalism Ambedkar wrote: "federalism was not the result of an agreement by the states to join in a federation.........no state has a right to secede from it"[11].

---

11 Austin (1966), p. 192.

It is arguable that on the whole Indian federalism negotiates and engages with language diversities well. One has to put it in a perspective to tease out Indian state's strategies of engagement. Although language issue is overtly emotive and symbolic, it would be wrong to confine it only to these levels. It is also strongly connected to jobs, business and power. It also provides a route through which ascending classes and elites can cement their rule by connecting to a larger constituency. In most places the language-based demands in India are usually elite-driven, and in a state where several language groups operate, one group may feel relatively marginalized. By creating a separate province based on a language, a linguistic minority of a larger unit can be converted into a political majority. This strategy diffuses inter-community tension and also brings specific groups closer to the realms of state power.

Indian federal experiences demonstrate that the goals different ethnic/ linguistic groups pursue are deeply connected to as well shaped by both 'politics of ideas' and 'politics of presence'[12]. This means an ethnic group not only wants their grievances to be redressed; they also believe that being a part of the group, they alone can represent its interest. However, intensity of ethnic mobilizations is only a part of the story. The other part is about the responses of the Indian state. Some scholars argue that it is a well institutionalized state and accommodative national leaders who tend to diffuse ethnic conflagration in India[13]. A well-institutionalized state not only allows ethnic groups to raise their demands, it also sets democratic limits within which they can do it. An accommodative national leadership that believes in sharing power and resources with other groups goes a long way in diffusing ethnic conflict. The rise and decline of Tamil nationalism in the 1950s and 1960s and of Sikh militancy in the 1980s and 1990s are often cited as cases to demonstrate the above hypothesis. At the same time the Muslim nationalism in Kashmir during the 1990s provides a good example of how an unaccommodating national leadership, weak institutionalization of democracy, recalcitrant militants supported by outside forces could push it on the path of repression and violence. Indian federalists believe that with a degree of 'self-rule' and accommodative attitudes of the national leadership, 'militancy' in Kashmir can be

---

12 Phillips, Anne (1995), The Politics of Presence, Oxford: Oxford University Press.

13 Kohli, Atul (2009), "Can Democracies Accommodate Ethnic Nationalism? Rise and Decline of Self-Determination Movements in India" in Democracy and Development in India: From Socialism to Pro-Business, New Delhi, Oxford University Press.

controlled.

If Federalism is a method of fostering shared-rule and self-rule[14] then India's democratic polity has tried to provide institutional embodiments to these values. As already mentioned, reorganization of states along linguistic lines was partly driven by the desire to provide self-rule to language groups. The creation of autonomous district and regional councils in the North East and Gorkhaland Territorial Administration in West Bengal can be seen also as facilitators of 'self-rule'.

The extent and the ways in which 'shared-rule' and 'self-rule' are mixed vary from one federal polity to the other. In a conventional reading, Indian federalism is often judged to the extent it deviates from an ideal federal doctrine or model. Anyone who considers the American federal model as the ideal type may view the Indian variant as a deviant. It is the 'lack' or the shortfall in India's federal system that then becomes the subject matter of discussion. This led some to view India's political system as unitary in spirit but federal in form. This is an unproductive methodological strategy. To see Indian federalism as entirely sue generis is also not helpful.

One of the productive ways would be to view India's federalism in the context of its history, and its changing character in the light of its embattled narratives of democracy. In terms of its specificities, Indian federalism is 'cooperative' and asymmetrical. Its goals are both functional (in terms of enhancing governance efficiency etc.) and cultural (a response to India's deep ethnic/ cultural diversity). The predominance of the Central government, as we have discussed before, is a product of its peculiar historical circumstances. The cooperative nature of India's federalism was largely premised upon addressing the goals of development, progress and stability. The Centre not only has to perform its role but also has to help the state governments to achieve common goals. The asymmetrical character was shaped by the ways in which independent India was crafted at the time of independence. The conditions of merger of certain sub-units prompted the constitution-makers to create special status for them. In order to preserve the special autonomy of Jammu and Kashmir within India, Article 370 was created. Similarly Article 371 provided special provisions for

---

14 Subrata K. Mitra and Malte Pehl, "Federalism", in Niraja Gopal Jayal and Pratap Bhanu Mehta (eds.), The Oxford Companion to the Politics in India (2010), Delhi: Oxford University Press.

the Nagas and Mizos in the North East, so that their customary laws could be protected. Maharashtra and Gujarat were allowed to establish separate developmental boards for their economically backward regions such as Vidarbha and Marathawada, Saurashtra and Kutch respectively. Similarly special provisions were enacted for Goa and Sikkim after their annexation to India. It is rightly argued that such asymmetry does not make India any less federal than the USA[15]. The upper house of the Indian Parliament, like the Senate of the USA, is designed to protect that interest of the sub-units. In the USA all the states are represented equally in the Senate. On the contrary, in India the states are represented according to their population. That means more populous states have more and less populous states have less members in the upper house. Some see this as positive, a demos-enabling feature of Indian federalism[16]. There are others who see in this system a potential for the smaller states to be dominated by the bigger states.

The force of 'post-partition' reality for which the Indian federalism took on a centralizing hue in the beginning subsided over time. But a smooth functioning of the federal polity in a relative sense was not entirely due to the intrinsic elements within India's federalism but because of certain contingent political circumstances of the time. The dominance of the Congress party at the federal and provincial levels, the quality of leadership exemplified by Nehru and the greater communication between the two levels kept the centralizing elements, for all practical purposes, dormant. With the passing away of Nehru, the relative decline of the Congress and greater mobilization of different class and caste groups at provincial levels, the functioning of the federal polity came under new pressure.

III

The pressure on the Indian federal polity need not be seen as something unnatural. At any rate the unfolding of democracy was supposed to bring in new pressure on the institutions of federal governance. In a sense, centralizing tendencies of the Union government and clamour for greater power by the states were always, continue to be, a function of politics in

---

15 Bhargava, Rajeev (2010), "The Evolution and Distinctiveness of India's Linguistic Federalism" in his The Promise of India's Secular Democracy, Delhi, Oxford University Press.

16 Bhargava, Rajeev (2010), p. 58.

India. As regional political parties emerged in the political horizon and the monopoly of the Congress declined in several Indian states, the stage was set for numerous battles between the federal Congress government and non-congress state governments. The unaccommodating nature of the Congress particularly during the reign of Indira Gandhi aggravated the process. The manipulative behavior of the federal government, the inappropriate use of emergency power particularly Article 356, the controversial role of Governor and the unequal financial relations became the source of much tension between the Centre and the states.

During 1951 to 1966 the President's rule (the Legislative Assembly suspended or dissolved by the President on the advice of the Governor) in the states as envisaged in Article 356 was declared on ten occasions. The next decade[17] (1967-1977) saw the number jumped to 41. During 1989 to 1997 the President's rule was imposed on thirteen occasions[18]. During the Constituent Assembly debates, Ambedkar while sharing the misgivings of some of the members about the 'emergency provisions' said "...that the proper thing we ought to expect is that such articles will never be called into question and they would remain a dead letter. If at all, they are brought into operation, I hope the President, who is endowed with all these powers, will take proper precautions before actually suspending the administration of provinces"[19].

It is quite clear from evidence that imposition of President's rule on many occasions was motivated by political considerations rather than by strict constitutional propriety. As the power of the regional non-Congress parties increased in the post-1967 election scenario, the voices against the centralizing power of the Union government were clearly heard. The federal discourse as a consequence moved in new directions. For instance,

---

17 Dhavan, Rajeev and Geetanjali Goel, "Indian Federalism and its Discontent: A Review" in Gert W Kueck, Sudhir Chandra Mathur and Klaus Schindler (eds.) (1998), Federalism and Decentralization: Centre-State Relations in India and Germany, New Delhi: Mudrit, p. 74-76.

18 Mitra, Subrata and Malte Pahle in The Oxford Companion to the Politics in India (2010).

19 M Siraj Sait, "Reorienting Federalism: Coming to terms with the Future" in Gert W Kueck, Sudhir Chandra Mathur and Klaus Schindler (eds.) (1998), p. 94.

the Rajamannar Commission[20] was set up in 1969 with direct support from the then Tamil Nadu Chief Minister Mr. Karunanidhi to look into the federal practices as enshrined in the Indian constitution. Predictably it suggested that Article 356 should be abolished in order to strengthen the relationship between the Centre and the states. A few years later in 1977 the Marxist government of West Bengal produced a memorandum on Centre-State relations. It argued that a strong "Centre can be an impediment to the promotion of regional democratic expressions. Hence devolution of powers may help ward off fissiparous tendencies instead of encouraging them"[21].

In the 1980s the mobilization of non-Congress parties on federal issues intensified. The rise of regional parties like Telugu Desam Party (TDP) in Andhra Pradesh, Assam Gana Parishad (AGP) in Assam, Akali Dal in Punjab, different splinter groups of Janata Dal, Kerala Congress in Kerala and AIDMK in Tamil Nadu created greater possibilities for articulating their concerns at the national level. In order to preempt the move of the opposition, Indira Gandhi appointed a Commission headed by a retired Supreme Court of India Mr. R. S. Sarkaria in 1983. The commission—popularly known as Sarkaria Commission - submitted its report in 1988. It contained 247 recommendations in order to strengthen the relationship between the Centre and the states. Unfortunately except for a couple of recommendations including the establishment of Inter State Council, nothing much has happened to these recommendations. Irrespective of political parties and coalitions, no government thus far has shown any real intent to implement the Sarkaria Commission's recommendations. The shot-lived National Front Government in the late 1980s and early 1990s also committed the same kind of mistakes while dealing with the state governments. It is not surprising to see how much of the federal discourse in India is caught up in bad faith.

The ascendency of regional parties in national arena is one of the significant political developments in India since the late 1990s. The demise of the Congress system and the inabilities of other national parties to fill the political vacuum means that for a foreseeable future the national politics would be coalitional. The efforts of Bharatiya Janata Party (BJP)

---

20 Saez, Lawrence (2002), Federalism without a Centre (The Impact of Political and Economic Reform on India's Federal System), New Delhi, Sage Publications.

21 Saez, Lawrence (2002), p. 39.

and the Congress would be to bring as many political parties to their fold as possible. The BJP-led National Democratic Alliance (NDA) government was propped up 14 regional parties. Similarly the United Progressive Alliance (UPA) government led by the Congress since 2004 enjoys the support of many regional parties.

Observers of Indian politics point out that in recent times, the 'theatre of politics has shifted to the states'. They argue that 'national electoral outcomes do not merely reflect the 'national mood' that prevails at that moment; rather they reflect an equilibrium of political forces that happens to obtain at the state level at the time when the national elections are called"[22]. What does the current political landscape holds for the future of India's federal polity? As political parties proliferate and regional parties join national coalition, will this reduce the centralizing impulse? As the process of economic liberalization proceeds further – by stealth or by open deliberations- will the competition for more FDI (Foreign Direct Investment) alter the ways states relate to each other and to the government at the Centre?

Not so long ago, the battle between the Centre and the states was essentially a battle between the National Congress and the regional parties. This is irretrievably changed. As the regional parties enjoy political power at the national level it is no more possible to see the national government as alien. The earlier anxiety that plagued the Centre-state relations has slowly died down. However, this will not be true in the case of some of the North Eastern States and Jammu Kashmir where the raw power of the Centre is clearly visible. In these places the Indian federal polity continues to remain not only unitary but also excessively coercive. Unfortunately, changing political configuration at the Centre in recent decades has not been able to break this deeply entrenched mould.

IV

India is deeply diverse and carries multiple cleavages in its social self. A federal polity, rather than a unitary one, is best suited to this fundamental

---

22 Yadav, Yogendra and Suhas Palshikar, "Revisiting 'Third Electoral System: Mapping Electoral Trends in India, 2004-2009", in Sandeep Shastri, K. C. Suri and Yogendra Yadav (eds.) (2009), Electoral Politics in Indian States, New Delhi: Oxford University Press, p. 395.

reality. India is also a land of much nationalism. Not all nationalisms are driven by the desire to establish an independent and sovereign state. A large number of them seek self-respect, dignity and autonomy. On the whole, Indian federalism has harnessed and tamed these sentiments and has given them a political space to operate. A federal polity also needs a common thread that can bind many groups and communities together. This can never be achieved by force. Nor can this be done with the aid of an exclusivist and majoritarian religious ideology. By tethering federalism to the narrative of democracy, India has tried to craft a tune for its citizens to hum individually and to sing in groups. The institutional forms that embody the federal idea must be strengthened; but only by keeping the larger objectives of democracy in mind. As pointed out earlier, federal idea gets diminished within a dyadic framework. It is in this context the need for meaningful decentralization must be emphasized.

Federalism is not a thick philosophical doctrine. But it is connected to the values of non-domination, equality and autonomy. But it is primarily a modus vivendi, a compromise, a desire for constituting and governing collective lives at different levels. From a legal point of view, federalism remains a part of India's 'basic structure', fundamental to its governance. It can't be easily altered by constitutional amendment. Just because it cannot be easily dumped cannot ensure its success. What can, however, is the desire to make it meaningful by making it respond to the changing realities of India. After all it must cohere with other valuable principles enshrined in the Indian constitution.

Re-Imagining Pakistan
Identity Politics in a National Security State

Ayesha Siddiqa

In the past four years of the political government elected in 2008, Pakistan seems to have shifted towards the concept of greater political autonomy of the federating units and in endorsing the principle of empowerment of ethnic communities. Such a move is reflected through the 18th amendment and the idea floated by the ruling Pakistan People's Party (PPP) to establish newer provinces that will be carved out of the politically powerful Punjab province.

In April 2010 the elected government of the Pakistan People's Party along with its coalition partners managed to pass the 18th amendment to the 1973 Constitution that allows for greater provincial autonomy as was envisioned by various national leaders, especially the former Prime Minister Zulfiqar Ali Bhutto. Pakistan being a multi-ethnic state with history of inter-ethnic strife, provincial autonomy that empowers the four main federating units and attached territories has been historically a much-contested issue. The lack of provincial autonomy during the 1960s had led to circumstances that propelled the dismemberment of East Pakistan in 1971. However, no real action was taken until very recently. The 18th amendment, however, was not an isolated act but it was an event which propelled yet another debate for the formation of newer provinces. This act would underscore the significance of ethnicity as a principle of political formation. Needless to say that this is not as smooth ailing as it sounds. Strengthening of the federation through provincial autonomy is considered as weakening of the one-nation idea by the powerful establishment of the Pakistani state.

After April 2010, when the PPP government introduced provincial autonomy, other issues have sprung up as well such as the demand for the creation of new provinces. The current focus seems to be Punjab which has traditionally dominated the politics of the state. The majority of the excessively powerful military and civil bureaucracy belongs to Punjab. Thus the demand for new province or provinces in Punjab, especially in the Southern part of the province seems to challenge the idea of the peculiar distribution of power. The idea of creating new provinces is not at all simple even though there may be evidence of this being a popular demand. The creation of a new political entity will have to maneuver massive resistance caused due to the chasm within the political landscape, opposing perception of the political leadership versus the military establishment, and, last but not the least, the tension between the political ideas of Pakistan versus the narrative of the national security state. My key argument is that the division of South Punjab is more than just a case study because a change in the physical boundaries of the most powerful region will determine a change in the mindset and attitude of the state. This means a major shift in the character of the state. Hence, a change will not happen until there is sufficient push from the inside that is the Saraiki region. To attain that, on the other hand, will require smoothening the differences and reaching at an understanding amongst the leadership of the Saraiki region.

The argument in this paper is that enhancement of national diversity and its acceptance in the form of provincial and ethnic autonomy is yet an incomplete project with results hard to achieve, especially in the short to medium term. My argument is that provincial autonomy may be an uphill task, but ethnic autonomy is even harder because the power elite of Pakistan is not primed to accept the concept. The creation of new projects, hence, will not be achieved until a serious political struggle is launched which seriously challenges the establishment political transformation. In this paper I will examine the ongoing debate regarding the establishment of new provinces with the objective of understating the tension within the state and the political system that makes the project of a new province impossible in the short to medium term, or even in medium to long term.

Re-Imagining Pakistan

In the 65th year of its birth Pakistan awaits being re-imagined. One of the critical issues worth attention pertains to improvement in distribution of resources through re-thinking its existing internal boundaries. In many respects this pertains to an existential threat faced by the state for which re-imagining may be a solution. There are whispers all over regarding the need for creating new provinces. While there is the demand for a province for the Urdu-speaking mohajirs (migrants from Muslim minority provinces in India) or another for the Pushtoons in Baluchistan, the more audible voices pertain to creating a Saraiki province in South Punjab. On its heels is the wish for the restoration of Bahawalpur province and even an idea of setting up a Hazara province in Northern Punjab. Although it is hard to imagine any of this wishes coming true in the foreseeable future, these demands seem to be spurred due to certain strategic and tactical policies of the current ruling coalition headed by the Pakistan People's Part Parliamentarian (PPPP). Strategically, the 18th amendment to the 1973 constitution and renaming of the North West Frontier Province to Khyber Pakhtunkhwa (KP) has changed political dynamics to the extent that it has made people in South Punjab and other sub-regions hopeful of getting their demands met. These constitutional changes seem to have shifted the emphasis of the state towards strengthening the federating units which was never the case in the past. Moreover, the aforementioned political actions have also highlighted the importance of ethnicity as a defining principle for the politics of the federation. Tactically, the ruling PPPP government seems to have expressed an interest in making more provinces in Punjab, certainly South Punjab. The biggest lacunae being that the ruling political party does not have any operational planning to make this happen. Ultimately, the intent of the state, the will of the political parties and internal political tensions at various levels will determine a way forward in this regard.

Re-imagining Pakistan through empowerment of the federating units and rationalizing the size of the existing units is not an anomaly since a similar exercise was carried out in India, a state with a similar history and made on the same formula as Pakistan. However, this is an extremely tricky project as far as Pakistan is concerned because some of the power centres are extremely suspicious of the proposed exercise for creating new provinces. There are three reasons for this. First, the powerful establishment considers re-imagining as an existential threat rather as a response to it. The national security state is deeply uncomfortable with altering the internal boundaries due to its imagination of domestic politics ultimately being captured and manipulated by external forces. Second, and this is connected to the first point, it is suspected that once the process of creating new units is set into motion, the formula will be applied all over the country which makes at least some of the political forces like the

Sindhi and Pushtoon leadership highly nervous. The Awami National Party (ANP), for instance, was critical of the demand for a Hazara province to be carved out from North Punjab and some territory currently in KP province. Such a demand came to surface in 2010 after the renaming of North West Frontier province to KP as part of the 18th amendment.

Third, the entire exercise of reformatting internal political boundaries looks like an effort that is currently focused on changing the political geography of the most powerful federating unit of the country. The smaller or minority provinces in Pakistan have historically been suspicious of the power of Punjab which is the largest unit in terms of the number of people. Prior to 1971 before East Pakistan succeeded from West Pakistan and became a separate state, a similar reservation was also expressed by the Bengali leadership of East Pakistan which was highly suspicious of centralization of power in West Pakistan, especially Punjab. Historically, the country's politically powerful military was predominantly Punjabi. Allegedly, until 2011 the military was 75 percent from Punjab, mainly a few districts of North and central Punjab. The same applies to the civil bureaucracy where Punjab has a higher representation mainly due to the quota system for selecting civil servants. Dividing Punjab into smaller units would serve the purpose of rationalizing the power political structure and also evenly divide power within the largest province where, for instance, South Punjabis feel that their interest would be better served through the formation of a separate province or provinces. Currently, South Punjab, which is also predominantly a rural area and relatively under-developed as compared to Central and north Punjab, does not have a separate quote and, hence, is not well represented in the civil bureaucracy or the armed forces. South Punjab is also known for lower standards of education and development.

From a development perspective there is a case for emphasizing establishing of a separate entity because South and North Punjab get lesser attention as compared to central Punjab. For instance, a glance at the development budget for the financial year shows that the highest share goes to Lahore. The district's development budget is about Rs 75 billion. This is in stark comparison to DG Khan's Rs. 20.6 billion, Bahawalpur's Rs 17.7 billion, Bahawalnagar's Rs 8.7 billion, or Bukkhur's Rs. 4.8 billion. Although smaller districts of North Punjab, as it is apparent from table 1 get lesser development budget, the state of South Punjab in comparative terms is the worst due to lack of development, higher incidence of poverty, lack of education and other factors. For instance, according to a report of the government of Punjab of year 2000, districts Rajanpur, Bahawalpur, Rahim Yar Khan, Muzaffargarh, Dera Ghazi Khan, Bahawalnagar and Lodhran, all in South Punjab, were the poorest in the entire province with a poverty figure of about 55 percent. The report also stated that the annual income of these districts was two to three times less than the affluent districts mostly located in Central or Northern Punjab. This finding was also subscribed to by a study conducted by the Lahore University of Management Science that put the incidence of poverty in South Punjab at 50.1 per cent, West Punjab at 52.1 per cent, Central Punjab at 28.76 percent, and North Punjab at 21.31 per cent. The poverty could be due to the varied economic patterns in different parts of Punjab. Agriculture is a dominant activity in South Punjab with almost 55 percent labour concentrated in this sector as opposed to 27 percent in North Punjab and 33 percent in central Punjab.[1] The fact is that most of the heavy manufacturing industry is concentrated in North and Central Punjab with relatively little industrialization in South and West Punjab. Most of the industry in the poverty-ridden regions is linked with agriculture.

However, there is a general lack of development in South and West Punjab, an issue also raised by the LUMS study that gauged the various districts of Punjab on the basis of a deprivation index that, in turn, was based on standard of education, housing quality, housing services (provision of utility services) and employment ratio. According to the report, districts such as Rahim Yar Khan in South Punjab ranked the lowest among the 34 districts of Punjab in the deprivation index. The other top 13 districts were also from South and West Punjab. Interestingly, the list of the least deprived districts included Rawalpindi Chakkwal, Lahore and Sialkot. The comparative condition of the various districts of Punjab on the basis of social indicators such as immunization, child mortality rate (under 5 yrs), ante-natal care, education and school enrollment also indicate some of the districts of South Punjab such as Rajanpur and Rahim Yar Khan ranking at the lowest as compared to some of the districts of Central and North Punjab. The percentage of boys that never enroll in school, for instance, was 30 percent for South Punjab, 27 percent for West Punjab, 12 percent for Central Punjab and 6 percent for North Punjab. In case of girls, the

---

1 Mansoor Ahmed, "Punjab tops in infant mortality, poverty, income inequality" in The News, 07/11/2008.

figure was 44 percent South Punjab, 44.5 percent West Punjab, 23 percent Central Punjab and 15 percent North Punjab.[2]

Politics of South Punjab

The development discrepancies might not have been noticed had it not been for a couple of noticeable developments in South Punjab. The first pertains to the rising tide of jihadism and religious extremism that some believe is caused due to poverty, underdevelopment and the nature of the political system in the sub-region. Muhammad Ali Durrani, the former information minister and the main voice behind the movement for the restoration of Bahawalpur province, was of the view that restoring the status of the former princely state as a province may give new direction to the youth and divert attention from the growing jihadism and radicalism in the area.[3] Poverty, indeed, is a contributory factor as far as jihadism is concerned and improvement in social and human indicators is likely to have an impact. However, the regional fiscal empowerment and reduction of radicalism is not linearly linked. Furthermore, radicalism may not even change with restoration for several reasons that do not fall in the purview of the present discussion.

Second and a more important factor pertain to the political rivalry between the two main national parties – PPPP and PML-N – over maintaining influence over the politically most influential region of the country. In aggregate terms the PPPP seems to have lost control over Punjab since the 1970s. The support in Punjab enjoyed by Bhutto gradually eroded but most specifically during and after the 1980s when General Zia's regime began establishing a leadership in Punjab as an alternative to the PPP in the form of Nawaz Sharif. After the 1988 elections the trend was obvious that while the PPP couldn't retain control of Central and North Punjab that moved away to the PML-N, Bhutto's party retained reasonable influence in South Punjab.[4] This is also the area with a large number of Saraiki speaking people. Although this is not a case of perfect polarization between the PML-N and the PPP as the former has some influence in the

---

2 Ibid.,

3 Discussion with Muhammad Ali Durrani (Islamabad: 2010).

4 Salman Tariq Kureshi, "Is the Party Over?" in Daily Times, 02/10/2010. http://www.dailytimes.com.pk/default.asp?page=2010   percent5C10   percent5C02 percent5Cstory_2-10-2010_pg3_2

urban centers of South Punjab, this is the only sub-region in province where the PPP can still hope to make electoral gains as compared to Central and North Punjab.

A combination of these two above described factors has resulted in greater visibility of the demand for a new province or provinces in the region.

Saraiki Province: New or Old Movement?

As mentioned earlier, the current Saraiki movement seems to draw its strength from particular forces. This not only includes the ruling PPP but also other parties such as the Mohajir Qaumi Movement (MQM) which would indirectly benefit from such re-imagining of the Pakistani state.[5] The party primarily representing the interests of the Urdu-speaking migrants eyes the Saraiki movement or any division of Punjab as a prerequisite for any metamorphosis of the state that would allow political representation to the MQM or legitimizes its political power. However, the main force behind the movement is the ruling PPP, which seems to be egging on the political movement at this juncture, despite that it may not have clarity regarding the issue. The Prime Minister Yusuf Raza Gillani announced the party's support for creating a new province in South Punjab.[6]

Such a support may have given renewed energy to the Saraiki movement, but it also gives the impression of this being a totally new political cause rater than an old issue as Saraiki nationalists would claim. The Saraiki national movement leadership's claim revolves around the claim regarding separate ethno linguistic identity of the Saraiki people which was initially ignored by the British and later by the Pakistani political leadership. Furthermore, they believe that since the Saraiki people have suffered subjugation since 1818 starting from Punjabi invasion by Maharaja Ranjeet Singh, they deserve political empowerment at this stage. Thus, the Saraiki nationalists see the movement beyond the issue of development discrepancy. It is claimed that Sariki is an important ethno-linguistic identity that was forcibly merged with Punjabi or ignored as

5 "MQM in Favor of Saraiki Province" in Dawn, 07/08/2011. http://www.dawn.com/2011/08/07/mqm-in-favour-of-saraiki-province.html

6 "Saraiki belt wants a separate province: Gillani" in The News, 04/03/2012. http://www.thenews.com.pk/article-38168-Saraiki-belt-wants-a-separate-province

part of the policy of the colonial powers and continues to be treated this way. Nukhbah Langah, for instance, in her scholarly work on the Saraiki movement has presented a case for the recognition of Sariki identity. She is of the view that the Saraiki people were denied their rightful place in Pakistan's political system and power politics despite that they formed a majority. This was done primarily through presenting Saraiki as a subset of Punjabi.[7] The argument regarding Saraiki merely being a dialect of Punjabi has resonance in North and Central Punjab. Such an argument presents the political bias of, what is considered as, the politically superior Punjabi identity and unwillingness to allow for the division of Punjab on the basis of ethno-linguistic identity. The PML-N leader Mian Nawaz Sharif, in fact, warned the prime Minister and the President to use the slogan for creating another province in Punjab responsibly[8] which effectively means not raising the issue at all.

Referring to the Saraiki movement, its intellectuals also claim that the urge for recognition of Saraiki as a separate identity and empowerment of its people is historic and indigenous, deeply set in the intellectual discourse of Sufi poets of the area like Khwaja Fareed who had implored the Nawab of Bahawalpur to rise above the subjugation of the British.

"Upnain mulk kun aap vasa tun

Put Ungreezi thane

(liberate your country

Uproot British police posts)"

The Nawab of Bahawalpur, Bahwal Khan III had signed an agreement with the British in 1833 that brought the state under British suzerainty giving it the right over the state's external relations and security. Thus, according to Langah's interpretation of Fareed's above-cited verse the Sufi poet implored the nawab, who was a Saraiki speaker, to free his community of people from external influence and intervention. Langah also offers samples from the more modern Saraiki poetry to support her case of Saraiki identity being popular among its people. Although the interpretation of Fareed's poetry as being nationalist in the sense that

---

7 Nukhnah Langah, *Poetry as Resistance: Islam and Ethnicity in Post-Colonial Pakistan* (New Delhi: Routledge, 2010). Pp. 7-30.

8 http://www.dailytimes.com.pk/default.asp?page=2012\03\06\story_6-3-2012_pg1_1

Langah has viewed it can be debated, the fact of the matter is that we can hear echoes of a movement definitely after the early 1970s. The former princely state of Bahawalpur had signed an instrument of accession with Pakistan in 1947. As part of the agreement it was given the status of a province and operated as one until it was merged into the one-unit scheme during the early 1950s. Contrary to the expectation of provincial status being restored after dissolution of the one-unit in the 1970s, Bahawalpur was merged into Punjab. At this point in time, the Bahawalpur movement, which according to a Pakistani scholar Umbreen Javaid, started during the 1960s and was mainly linguistic-cultural in nature turned political as well.[9] In 1970 it turned violent as well when General Yahya Khan's regime opted to use force against the protestors resultantly killing a few who are to date remembered as 'martyrs of Bahawalpur'. The movement, as opposed to the present day movement for the restoration of Bahawalpur province, had a deeper Saraiki character. It was not just an issue of not restoring Bahawalpur's status as a province but denoted the anxiety of the indigenous Saraiki population regarding the impact of migration into Saraiki speaking areas due to the 'colonization of land' scheme that brought in settlers from other parts of the country, mainly Central and North Punjab into these areas.[10] Unfortunately, such an activity has continued to happen with the land in the Cholistan desert in Bahawalpur being distributed to people from other parts of the country under the Punjab Colonization of Land Act 1912 and beyond. For instance, the army, in which the Saraiki people have hardly any share, tends to usurp land and distribute it or lease it out to its personnel and cronies. They even steal water for irrigation.[11] Saraiki nationalists are of the view that even leaders like Zulfiqar Ali Bhutto, who promised support for the cause on his visit to the area, but totally followed a different policy when he went to Lahore, made a criminal compromise with the Central Punjabi lobby on the issue.[12]

However, it is important to see the Bahawalpur movement of the 1960s up until 1971, when it succumbed to brutal state pressure, was

9   Umbreen Javaid, " Movement for Bahawalpur Province" P. 44. http://pu.edu.pk/ images/journal/pols/Currentissue-pdf/Movement percent20for percent20Bahawalpur percent20Province.pdf

10   Ibid.,

11   Ayesha Siddiqa, "The Real Culprits" in Newsline, 15/02/2011. http://www. newslinemagazine.com/2011/02/the-real-culprits/

12 Interview with Abdul Majeed Kanjo (Islamabad: 10/12/2009).

loosely linked with the Saraiki identity issue. The members elected to the National Assembly and the Punjab provincial assembly from the area in the 19790s elections had all won on the basis of their demand for the Bahawalpur province. In fact, Bahawalpur was one area where the PPP, which was dominant in the rest of Punjab, could not make any inroads as it had deserted the cause. More important, the elected members were predominantly Saraiki but it included Punjabis as well which basically denotes that the population at large was anxious about the area that was historically the state of Bahawalpur with some consideration for the language but not an over-emphasis on the issue.

Does this mean that the Saraiki people were not keen then for recognition of their separate ethno-linguistic identity? The fact of the matter is that the identity issue, which seems to have become audible now, was historically more of a whisper due to two reasons. First, historically, South Punjab was ruled, as mentioned earlier, by 'foreign' forces that had an impact on political behavior and in hampering consciousness of separate ethno-linguistic identity. It also meant that the people were unable to consolidate protest until there was an opportune moment to do so. During Ranjeet Singh's era, for instance, even the Saraiki speakers had begun to speak Punjabi under influence of the ruler. Subsequently, the British on capturing Multan and the adjoining areas lumped it as part of Punjab. Second, the Saraiki elite, which aught to have raised the issue continued to appease the Punjabi elite and even the British rulers for sake of getting their share of power.

It has taken years for the development of the Saraiki consciousness but it seems to be gradually ripening, especially in view of the development discrepancies between the indigenous Saraiki populace and other ethnicities in South Punjab.[13] The local population is increasingly conscious of the fact that bureaucrats from Central and North Punjab have acquired assets and have access to resources of the land which the local population cannot get. For instance, senior civil and military bureaucrats not only get land but also access to a scare resource – water.[14] Notwithstanding the inability of the leadership to develop human resources, the average Saraiki lags behind other ethnicities in

---

13 Rasul Bakhsh Rais, "Southern Punjab's Troubles" in The Daily Times, 16/06/2009.

14 Ayesha Siddiqa, *Military Inc: Inside Pakistan's Military Economy.* (London: Pluto Press, 2007). P. 185.

South Punjab and has become conscious of the disparity, especially between the mohajir and Saraiki and Punjabi and Saraki. This is bound to give rise to a certain kind of politics which will demand recognition of the distinct ethno-linguistic identity of the Saraiki people rather than just being a subject of interest due to the relative backwardness of the indigenous people, an example of feudalism or as an exotic culture which is showcased in a peculiar way by a Central Punjabi dominated media.[15] Intriguingly, even the Saraiki channels are managed and run by Central and North Punjabis than Saraikis themselves. The control of media is being cursorily mentioned to make a larger point about the clash of narrative: the politically powerful Punjabi narrative versus the relatively weak yet emerging Saraiki narrative.

Restoration of Bahawalpur Province

The non-acceptance of the Saraiki narrative is probably one of the reasons for the emergence of the movement for the restoration of Bahawalpur province right on the heels of the re-emergence of the Saraiki movement post-2008. Some view it as a conspiracy due to the kind of people involved in the movement such as the former information minister Muhammd Ali Durrani, who has never had any sympathy for Bahawalpur in the past, no emotional affinity for the area or done anything for its betterment.[16] Many believe that Durrani is compelled by his need to find a constituency in the area as he is out of depth as far as electoral politics is concerned. If the idea materializes it would certainly give Durrani a fillip politically. He believes that Bahawalpur province is more of a possibility because, unlike Saraiki province, Bahawalpur just needs to be re-created. Therefore, with the strategic use of the media Durrani and his allies, most of whom currently find themselves on the margins of power politics; have partly diverted attention away from an ethno-linguistic issue to an administrative matter. This also means a deep chasm within the Saraiki movement as Bahawalpur is critical of Saraiki province.

The Durrani-led Bahawalpur province movement is focused on

15 Nukhbah Langah, "Siraiki Drama Programming on PTV: the Concept of 'Backwardness' through a Postcolonial Lens" in ELF, Annual Research Journal Vol. 13, 2011 (Khairpur, Sindh: Journal of the Department of English, Shah Abdul Latif Bhittai University). Pp. 21-35.

16 http://waseb.wordpress.com/2010/04/19/south-punjab-movement-by-ayesha-siddiqa/

streamlining the differences amongst the Saraiki elite. They raise fear amongst Bahawalpur's leadership and general public of dominance by the Saraiki leaders in case the capital of the new Saraiki province is Multan. I had a chance of conducting a sample survey (600 people) in Bahawalpur of various ages that aimed at comprehending people's understanding of why it is necessary to have a Bahawalpur province. Based on the results of the sample it can be argued that not all people in Bahawalpur are convinced of the efficacy of Bahawalpur province. And those that do are interested for sake of better economic opportunities (see table 1).

Table 1

People's Responses to Bahawalpur Province		
1	**Do you want a Bahawalpur Province?**	
	Yes	60 %
	No	40 %
2	**How will a province impact your life?**	
	Positive:	
2(a)	New job opportunities:	20 %
2(b)	Bahawalpur will develop	15 %
2 ©	Will get separate budget	5 %
2(d)	Water problem will get solved	5 %
2(e)	Cost of living will be cheaper	40 %
2(f)	Increase in education	25 %
	Negative:	
2(g)	No impact	45 %
2(h)	Increase in terrorism	55 %
3	**Do you know the leadership of the movement?**	
	Yes	56 %
	No	44 %
4	**Do you trust these leaders?**	
	Yes	57 %
	No	43 %

Historically, major strides in infrastructure development were made during the time of the princely state which people remember, especially the Saraiki population of the area. Therefore, a general perception is that an independent province would bring back progress of the past.[17] The leadership of the Bahawalpur province movement seems unwilling to examine the current socioeconomic realities of Bahawalpur especially the fact that a region, which was financially viable 60 years ago, might not be in the same condition since it has larger population and less industrialization than other parts of Punjab and even South Punjab.

The Central Punjabi leadership exploits such differences to its advantage and has resorted to methods to checkmate the movement through supporting other ideas such as dividing Punjab into three administrative divisions: North, Central and South, or support the movement for the restoration of Bahawalpur province (there will be greater details on this issue in the next sub-section). Other Punjab based parties, such as the PML-Q also seem to have followed the formula for establishing administrative units rather than put their effort more seriously behind the Saraiki movement. The reason for this being that the PML-Q leadership is from Central and North Punjab and susceptible to the traditional bias of the Central Punjabi vis-à-vis other ethnicities. This is a critical pressure on the current PPP government due to its political coalition with the PML-Q. Nonetheless, the PPP under the leadership of Asif Zardari seems to offer a challenge to the PML-N by negotiating under the table deals with the nawab of Bahawalpur and by offering to make Bahawalpur as the capital of the new Saraiki or South Punjab province. The under the table negotiations include personal benefits to the nawab and his family which is critical for the Bahawalpur province movement.[18] The idea of throwing bait to both the movement leadership and the nawab family is indeed an intelligent move to checkmate subversive elements who insist on a separate Bahawalpur province only with the intention of blocking a South Punjab province.

The Politics of Re-Imagining

At this juncture the most important question worth asking is if re-imagining is possible at all? But before one attends to this issue a subsidiary question is that what shape would this re-imagination take?

---

17 Yaqoob Khan Bangash, "Remembering Bahawalpur Province" in Express Tribune, 06/02/2012.

18 "Covert Understanding: Nawab Drops Demand for Bahawalpur Province". In Express Tribune, 02/08/2012. http://tribune.com.pk/story/416237/covert-understanding-nawab-drops-demand-for-bahawalpur-province/

The Saraiki and Bahawalpur province issues are highly critical in mapping the re-imagining of Pakistan because if either happens it will determine the future possibilities for other ethnic communities that hope to expand their political spaces within the Pakistani federation. For instance, the success of either the Saraiki or Bahawalpur province would then legitimize creation of Hazara province in North Punjab and Southern KP or even a province for the mohajirs in urban Sindh which is certainly a more emotionally explosive issue. The two movements in Punjab are critical as the province is considered as the repository of state power. Thus the internal political bifurcation of Punjab is a necessary barometer to assess the attitude of the state and its establishment towards the issue of re-imagining the country.

The very fact that creation or re-creation of provinces is being discussed indicates a new attitude amongst the public of various areas that want their ethnic identities included in the state's redistributive system. The creation of a new state in 1947 based on a social contract between the then accepted four ethno-linguistic categories laid the foundation of not only a new federation but of a principle of the primacy of ethnic identities. The four categories accepted at the time of partition were the ones recognized by the withdrawing colonial forces which did not mean that others could not re-negotiate their share at a future point in time.

However, the process of re-negotiating internal boundaries on the basis of ethno-linguistic identity or on the basis of administrative viability is an uphill task as stipulated in art 239 (4) question of the 1973 Constitution. According to this rule, no bill to amend the constitution with the objective of changing provincial boundaries can be presented to the President for approval unless passed by two-thirds majority of the provincial assembly concerned and two-thirds majority in both the houses of the Parliament.[19] It goes without saying that the underlying assumption is that once there is a genuine need for redefining political boundaries the will of the majority will prevail upon the parliamentarians. Nonetheless, given the nature of Pakistan's politics this is a stupendously difficult process. More important, even if various stakeholders agree on further sub-divisions the important question is that what formula will they be likely to adopt? This is not a simple question rather the

19 "The Issue of New Provinces" See, http://apnaorg.com/articles/punjab-division/times-of-pakistan/

answer is based on the fundamentals of the nature of the state.

In some respects Muhammad Ali Durrani's claim regarding the strength of the idea of restoring Bahawalpur province vis-à-vis creating Saraiki province holds water as the permanent establishment in Pakistan is not entirely comfortable with the idea of an ethno-linguistic identity. While I will return to this debate later, it is suffice to say at this moment that there may be greater acceptance amongst the establishment of the idea of administrative divisions which are essentially ethnic neutral, like Bahawalpur. A glance at table 2 shows the ethnic makeup of Bahawalpur and all other areas that the Saraiki national movement would like to be included in Saraikistan.

Table 2

Population By Mother Tongue -- 1998 Census

Name of District	Total	Urdu	Punjabi	Sindhi	Pushto	Balochi	Saraiki	Others
1	2	3	4	5	6	7	8	9
Bahawalpur	2,433,091	132,679	690,750	2,940	13,609	1,814	1,565,318	25,981
Bahawalnagar	2,061,447	77,201	1,950,368	238	6,033	440	24,692	2,475
Bhakkar	1,053,456	77,665	183,481	465	13,387	397	767,530	10,531
DG Khan	1,643,118	52,993	21,138	1,454	11,310	235,445	1,318,628	2,150
DI Khan	852,995	27,786	7,797	474	187,857	400	618,147	10,534
Khanewal	2,068,490	161,069	1,679,988	1,089	23,263	650	120,730	81,701
Layyah	1,120,951	35,252	364,904	1,126	16,938	615	697,810	4,306
Lodhran	1,171,800	106,788	216,854	1,191	2,778	177	815,829	28,183
Mianwali	1,056,620	37,361	783,775	1,388	105,175	129	126,342	2,450
Multan	3,116,851	494,269	674,438	2,208	19,301	3,091	1,891,095	32,449
Muzaffargarh	2,635,903	129,862	195,526	2,139	24,218	3,473	2,271,420	9,265
Rahim Yar Khan	3,141,053	90,910	857,718	62,632	23,106	35,466	1,967,126	104,095
Rajan Pur	1,103,618	35,728	36,882	716	5,322	188,352	835,747	871
Vehari	2,090,416	108,429	1,731,926	466	4,293	595	237,349	7,358
Sahiwal	1,843,194	26,083	1,807,659	472	6,485	568	1,489	438

Name of District	Total	Urdu	Punjabi	Sindhi	Pushto	Balochi	Saraiki	Others
Sargodha	2,665,979	155,598	2,487,002	381	17,449	791	2,558	2,200
Khushab	905,711	13,407	876,745	475	6,063	287	5,763	2,971
Jhang	2,834,545	94,061	2,717,147	959	13,099	319	3,955	5,005
Tank	238,216	1,567	369	72	191,334	35	44,108	731

Source: Bureau of Statistics, Islamabad

It is noticeable that the Saraiki-speakers are not in dominant number in one of the districts – Bahawalnagar. Moreover, from a power political perspective Bahawalpur has turned ethnic neutral as the key players are not only Saraikis but Punjabis and mohajirs as well. In fact, Punjabis and mohajirs represent the new capitalist class in Bahawalpur that seems to have overtaken the traditional wealth of the Saraiki landlord in the area. Tariq Bahsir Cheema, who is a Punjabi settler and a prominent politician, has redistributed resources strategically in areas where his ethnic community is in larger numbers, dominates the politics of district Bahawalpur, which is one of the three districts of Bahawalpur division. The Saraiki nationalists also suggest a problem in Bahawalpur movement from the perspective of this representing the sentiments of the Saraiki people. The fact is that the current leadership of the movement differs from that of the 1970s since a lot of the new leaders were opposed to the idea in the past.

Although Bahawalpur province is as much of a distant possibility as any other idea, comparatively it is more likely to happen due to this being ethnic neutral as compared to the Saraiki and Hazara provinces or that for the Urdu-speaking mohajirs in Sindh. If one were to look at a state-centric perspective as presented by scholars like Rasul Bakhsh Rais that undermine the project of creating new provinces and rubbish the idea on the basis that the pattern of migration in the past 65 years does not allow for such development, it is clear that the establishment has little patience for the project of making new provinces. However, an ethnic-potent concept is a complete non-starter as far as the permanent power in the country is concerned.

Clearly then, Saraiki province is more of a difficult venture due to four reasons.

First, the Saraiki movement may not really take off as long as it continues to define itself primarily from a development perspective. Since 2008, the basic reaction of the PML-N government, or before this the PML-Q government, is to distribute resources or add a few more millions in the development fund for the area every time they were confronted with protest regarding excessive power being exercised by Lahore that is the seat of political power in Punjab. A glance at table 3 will show that there is truth in these allegations as far as the discrepancy in allocations and expenditure between some large cities of central and north Punjab versus south is concerned.

Table 3

Punjab: A Comparison for Income & Expenditure, FY-2010/2011			
District	**Final Budget**	**Actual Expenditure**	**Population (1998 Census)**
North Punjab			
DIST GOVT ATTOCK	5008583245	7602872504	1,274,935
DIST GOVT CHAKWAL	4339230235	6563458405	1,083,725
DIST GOVT CHINIOT	2329754771	3655225950	
DIST GOVT MANDI BAHUDDIN	2575016158	5512910028	1,160,552
DIST GOVT GUJRAT	4995594424	10754497465	2,048,008
DIST GOVT JHELUM	2915497649	5301188887	936,957
DIST GOVT RAWAL PINDI	7750582820	14073584608	3,363,911
DIST GOVT SIALKOT	6385977228	12489286803	2,723,481
Central Punjab			
DIST GOVT FAISALABAD	12854526559	24198341880	5,429,547
DIST GOVT GUJRANWALA	8589433927	13746580631	3,400,940
DIST GOVT HAFIZABAD	2608450434	4452472936	832,980

Punjab: A Comparison for Income & Expenditure, FY-2010/2011

District	Final Budget	Actual Expenditure	Population (1998 Census)
DIST GOVT KASOOR	6129396466	8605562117	2,375,875
DIST GOVT NANKANA SAHB	3427687125	6313212566	
DIST GOVT NAROWAL	4004032281	7575636967	1,265,097
DIST GOVT SHEIKHUPURA	5437074757	20240434930	3,321,029
DIST GOVT TOBA TEK SINGH	3860124656	7307971076	1,621,593
DISTRICT GOVT LAHORE	14488439135	23304939325	6,318,745
South Punjab			
DIST GOVT OKARA	5735534261	8579871042	2,232,992
DIST GOVT JHANG	5071887315	9998842004	2,834,545
DIST GOVT BAHAWALPUR	6210845396	10952793906	2,433,091
DIST GOVT BHAWAL NAGUR	6629324834	13619178723	2,061,447
DIST GOVT BHUKKAR	3946591262	6028325392	1,051,456
DIST GOVT D.G. KHAN	4301342793	11717487038	1,643,118
DIST GOVT KHANIWAL	4986776879	10297910103	2,068,490
DIST GOVT KHUSHAB	3607340248	5470815236	905,711
DIST GOVT LAYYAH	4206319002	6795215962	1,120,951
DIST GOVT LODHRAN	4093397151	5761761253	1,171,800
DIST GOVT MIANWALI	3678935686	6549834094	1,056,620
DIST GOVT MULTAN	7650215117	12434127910	3,116,851
DIST GOVT MUZZAFFAR GHAR	5410087636	9802177894	2,635,903
DIST GOVT PAK PATTAN	3152457084	5399002491	1,286,680

Punjab: A Comparison for Income & Expenditure, FY-2010/2011			
District	Final Budget	Actual Expenditure	Population (1998 Census)
DIST GOVT RAHIM YAR KHAN	7336867923	11981069681	3,141,053
DIST GOVT RAJANPUR	2727091000	5172425222	1,103,618
DIST GOVT VEHARI	5824788349	6113499855	2,090,416
DIST GOVT SAHIWAL	4834463679	8823749240	1,843,194
DIST GOVT SARGODHA	6236759567	13387801927	2,665,979
Figures in Rs billion			
Source: Controller-General of Accounts, Islamabad			

The skeptics would, however, argue that the discrepancy is due to the difference in the number of people living and income generation capacity of each district. An argument could also be made after looking at the above figures that some of the large cities of South Punjab may not compare with larger districts like Lahore, Faisalabad and Rawalpindi, but these were not doing too poorly either. The counter argument also challenges allegations of kleptocratic distribution of resources by claiming that the lack of development in South Punjab is caused due to continued feudalism in the sub-region.[20] This argument holds some water, as those who possess capital in the area have not really invested in industrial growth even though that they may claim lack of indulgence by policy makers from Central and North Punjab. But development alone may be a limited perspective to analyze the critical question of how linguistic-ethnic identity determines political power and whether its significance needs to be re-established in re-imagining Pakistan. In any case, there are other aspects as well which must be considered in reviewing the distribution of resource debate such as the representation of people from South Punjab in the civil and military bureaucracy, two institutions which dominate the state and its power politics. Notwithstanding the relatively poor level of education and literacy in South Punjab, the people of this area suffer even more due to being tagged along with Central and North Punjab that has the

20   Rasul Bakhsh Rais, "Southern Punjab's Troubles: in Daily Times, 16/06/2009.

bulk of industry and is socioeconomically more developed. While areas with similar socioeconomic conditions like Baluchistan and Sindh (rural) have benefitted due to allocation of separate quota in the civil service, such a benefit has not accrued to South Punjab (see table 4). Similarly, military inductions have shown a bias for North and Central Punjab as compared to the South.[21]

Table 4

FPSC Provincial Merit	
Provinces	**Merit Percentage**
Punjab (incl. Federal Capital)	50 percent
Sindh	19 percent
Sindh (Urban)	40 percent of 19 percent
Sindh (Rural)	60 percent of 19 percent
KP	11.50 percent
Baluchistan	6 percent
GB/FATA	4 percent
AJK	2 percent
Source: Federal Public Service Commission	

Second, emotionally the society at large does not seem prepared to re-negotiate boundaries amongst its various segments. Creating new provinces is bound to open up a pandora's box as a number of communities have an overlapping settlement pattern. For instance, Saraiki nationalists visualize a province that includes a couple of districts of KP as well such as D.I. Khan and Tank (see map). The ANP leadership has already decried MQM's support for the idea of creating new provinces.[22] Although this objection was in reference to the creation of Hazara province, there is little possibility that the same leadership would approve of taking away of its districts for inclusion in another province. This is not to argue that newer provinces on ethno-linguistic basis cannot be created but that the likelihood of those that oppose the idea exploiting inter-societal differences and emotional insecurities of various communities may be a huge barrier.

---

21 C. Christine Fair and Shuja Nawaz, "The Changing Pakistan Army Officer's Corps" in Pp. 17-23).

22 "MQM, ANP exchange barbs over new provinces" in Daily Times, 04/01/2010.

Third, considering Punjab's dominance of the country's power politics the idea will be resisted fiercely out of fear of reducing the size and influence of what is currently the largest province. Despite that the Central Punjab dominated PML-Q seem to support the idea of three provinces, it is basically to rollback the idea than bankroll it.

Finally, the most important explanation is the nature of the state itself which does not allow for newer divisions. Nukhbah Langah has very correctly pointed out the colonial political attitude of the state and its power establishment that is highly uncomfortable with giving credence to ethno-linguistic identity politics.[23] Time and again, the Pakistani state has demonstrated a discomfort with ethnic politics and desires to snub it with force. Be it the Bengali, the Baluch or the Saraiki identity, the national security state relates to these identities in terms of foreign manipulation and this being a tool for unraveling Pakistan. The centrist-national security state would rather have a common identity or centrally-defined 'Pakistaniat' which it has tried to achieve through encouraging Islamic

---

23 Nukhnah Langah, *Poetry as Resistance: Islam and Ethnicity in Post-Colonial Pakistan* (New Delhi: Routledge, 2010). Pp. 7-30.

ethos to work as a gel.

Some people also link the tension in Sindh urban with the establishment's discomfort with the idea of division of Punjab. It is believed that the wall-chalking in some of the bigger cities of Sindh including Karachi regarding the demand for a South Sindh province, which it is assumed will be dominated by the mohajir community, was not just an innocent political act but a suspicious activity carried out to put pressure on the ruling PPP government. With the threat of its political position being undermined in Sindh the PPP may give up the idea of dividing Punjab. For the PPP, on the other hand, the slogan of creating a new province even if it does not manage to implement the idea is critical in its next electoral battle versus the key party from Punjab, the PML-N. It hopes to use the slogan to attract more votes. However, whether it managed to create a Saraiki or South Punjab province is a tremendous challenge. The PML-N leadership recently questioned PPP's sincerity. It was of the view that the Parliamentary commission for making of new provinces did not comprise of the right kind of members and the opposition was not taken on board.[24]

In short, the project of making new provinces in Pakistan, especially those based on ethno-linguistic identity denotes a tension between the western notion of nation-state and the emotional and political values of various communities that live in the land.

Conclusion

A Saraiki nationalist was perhaps more hopeful of getting a province a couple of years ago than now. This is due to the suspicion of the ongoing discourse on creating new provinces being more of an electoral ploy than anything substantive. Perhaps there is some truth in such suspicion as creating a new province is an existential issue for both the communities affected by it and the national security state which is highly nervous about the impact the process of internal political divisions may have on state's stability.

The centrist forces, which dominate power politics, are not inclined to rationalize the state structure for fear of what it may mean for the health of the state. An impression is being created regarding new provinces being

---

24 "New Provinces: PML-N Rejects Makeup of Parliamentary Panel:. In Express Tribune, 18/08/2012 http://tribune.com.pk/story/423678/new-provinces-pml-n-rejects-make-up-of-parliamentary-panel/

a difficult task on the grounds that no single territory purely represents one particular ethnicity and that tabling the issue may open a pandora's box. Indubitably, re-imagining the state is a difficult task and requires maturely negotiating at several levels. This can be achieved through agreeing upon a formula that allows for newer entities and recognition of the emotional and political needs of people. It is vital to understand that creating new provinces may not necessarily fuel inter-communal tension or damage the country, but accommodate multiple identities within the political structure of the state. It is about giving groups a sense of ownership in the state for which there seems little appetite.

CHT Regional Council: Regional Autonomy within Unitary System of Bangladesh

-Abdur Rob Khan[1]

Introduction

Regional autonomy brings into context the concept of federal system, which in Political Science, is a model of distribution of power between the centre and the constituent federating units.[2] Federal system allows certain degree of autonomy to a federating state in deciding its local laws and addressing development needs. Local laws can be modified according to local needs and demands. Another advantage is the simplification in governance achieved through the distribution of power and jurisdiction between the centre and state.[3] This distribution is a dialectical process. Federalism evolves over time through trials and errors and variants of regional autonomy emerge in the process. For example, within the Indian federal system, the Chakma Autonomous Hill District in Mizoram[4] evolved in a bid to protect the special needs and identity of the Chakma populace. Thus, the Chakma Hill Districts may be said to enjoy double autonomy, one as part of the Indian federal union, second as a special case under Schedule 6 of the Indian Constitution. Pertinent question is: how autonomous are such special cases when the polity is a unitary one? The present article is a case in point in the context of Chittagong Hill Tracts (CHT), the region of south east tip of Bangladesh comprising the three

---

1 Associate Professor of International Relations, North South University, Dhaka. Paper presented at Regional Seminar on "South Asia: Nation Building and Federalism" organized by Nepal Centre for Contemporary Studies (NCCS), Kathmandu, 26-27 August, 2012.

2 See, R.C. Agarwal, *Political Theory,* New Delhi: S. Chand and Company Ltd. 2007: 286-300.

3 Omkar Phatak, 'Federal System", in http://www.buzzle.com/articles/federal-system. html, accessed on August 12, 2012.

4 See, "An Inception of Chakma Autonomous Hill District" in https://sites.google.com/ site/voiceofjummaland/cadc-mizoram, accessed on August 9, 2012.

Hill districts: Rangamati, Bandarban and Khagrachari.

Bangladesh is a unitary state over a territorial space of 143,99,889 square km. The territory is divided into 64 districts with an average size of 0.22 m sq km and an average population of 2.5 million. Although the country got independence in the process of fighting for regional autonomy between the two wings of the then united Pakistan, on independence, the country opted for unitary system, given its small and compact size and more or less homogenous population. However, right from the beginning of the nation building process including framing of the Constitution in 1972, a minority section of the populace, namely, the Hill people of the Chittagong Hill Tracts, dissented with the nationality question on the ground they have a separate ethno-religious and linguistic identity, different from the mainstream Bengali nation. They also demanded regional autonomy for the Hill tribes, including 'excluded status' which was granted to them by the British colonial rulers.[5] As the demand was not accommodated in the new Constitution of Bangladesh adopted in November 1972, the movement of the Parbattya Chattacgram Jana Sanghati Samity (Chittagong Hill Tracts People's Association), the body spearheading the autonomy demand, eventually snowballed into a full-fledged insurgency in the latter part of the 1970s for a separate homeland, called Jumma Land[6]. The Government responded with counter-insurgency measures as well as negotiations that persisted through the 1980s and better part of 1990s. In the meantime, international dimensions to the problem were added with exodus of tribal refugees to Mizoram, and later, in Tripura, in India, on the one hand, and Bangladesh's perception and allegation that the CHT insurgents were trained and armed by India.

Eventually, an Accord was signed with the insurgents, known as Shanti Bahini, in 1997 under which the refugees from India returned, the Shanti Bahinis laid down arms and a Regional Council along with three autonomous Hill Districts were created. The strategic aspect of the insurgency was solved, ground for meeting their key demand, namely, regional autonomy, was created. However, full implementation of the Accord, namely, rehabilitation of refugees, sorting out land disputes and

---

5   The Regulation is known as "The Chittagong Hill Tracts Regulation 1900" or 1900 Manual, in short. See, its reproduction in http://www.satp.org/satporgtp/countries/ bangladesh/document/actandordinances/chittagon_hill.htm, accessed August 22, 2012.

6   'Jumma' comes from 'Jum', the slash and burn cultivation method practiced for ages by the Hill people.

agreed demilitarization of the CHT has not taken place.

The focus of the present paper is on the issue of regional autonomy within a unitary system. However, the degree of autonomy hinges on the nature of agreement and its implementation. Thus, implementation of the Accord will also be touched upon. However, since in a unitary system, traditional scope of autonomy comes from local government system, a brief profiling of the local government system in Bangladesh is provided first. Secondly, back grounding of the CHT insurgency as a run up to the Accord in 1997 is made. The Third section makes a critical assessment of the Regional Council. Fourth section reviews the lacuna in implementation of the Accord. The assessments of the stakeholders regarding the Regional Council will be contrasted to how far the Accord is likely to be implemented. Some recommendations are made in conclusion.

Local Government System in Bangladesh

This section intends to review the degree of autonomy and self-governing character of the local government system in Bangladesh. The country has a chequered history of local government system. Article 9 of the fundamental principles of state policy in the Constitution of Bangladesh states: The State shall encourage local Government institutions composed of representatives of the areas concerned and in such institutions special representation shall be given, as far as possible, to peasants, workers and women.[7] Chapter III on Local Government in the Constitution goes into some details about the purpose and methodology of building up a system of local government in the country. For example, Article 60 of Chapter III states: Parliament shall by law confer power on the local government bodies referred to in that article [Article 59], including power to impose taxes for local purposes, to prepare their budgets and to maintain funds.[8]

Local government institutions in Bangladesh are of two types: urban local government and rural local government or the rest of the country.

Urban Local Government

Traditionally, urban local governments are known as municipalities or

---

7   See, *The Constitution of the People's Republic of Bangladesh [as modified upto 30th April 1996],* Government of Bangladesh, Part II, p. 5.

8   Ibid.

Pourashavas. To qualify as municipality, minimum population of an urban centre has to be 15000, 75 percent of the population being engaged in non-farm occupation and a population density of no less than two thousand per sq km. Total number of urban centres in Bangladesh, as of national census 1991 was 522 of which number of municipalities was 138.[9] However, present number of municipalities has gone up to 269. Bigger cities, particularly, seven Divisional Headquarters, with metropolitan police administration are given City Corporation status. Recently, the capital city has been divided into two city corporations – North Dhaka and South Dhaka. The urban local government bodies are staffed with elected representatives since independence. Only exception has been the city corporations in the capital city where elections remain pending for the last three years.

The functions of Pourashavas and City Corporations are basically similar. The 1997 Pourashavas Ordinance categorized the functions of Pourahsavas as compulsory and optional. The mandatory functions include: construction and maintenance of roads, bridges and culverts; removal, collection and disposal of refuse; provision and maintenance of street lighting; provision of street watering; provision and regulation of water supply; establishment and maintenance of public markets; plantation of trees on road sides; maintenance and regulation of sanitation system; prevention of infectious diseases and epidemics; registration of births, deaths and marriages; provision and maintenance of slaughter houses; provision and maintenance of drainage; control over the construction and reconstruction of buildings; provision and maintenance of graveyards and burning places; control over traffic and public vehicles[10]

Many of the municipalities have only nominal existence with rudiments of urban facilities. Main problem is budgetary constraints. Operationally, the municipalities, city corporations, in particular, suffer from overlapping responsibilities of multiple authorities resulting in a chaotic situation. Thirdly, like all other local bodies in the countries, municipalities are not allowed autonomy by the central government. City Corporations mayors,

---

9 N. Islam,. M. Chatterjee and Y. Kaizong (eds.), *Urban and Regional Development in Bangladesh: Past Trends and Future Prospects*, Regional Science in Developing Countries, London, 1997. M. M. Khan,, *Urban Local Governance in Bangladesh: an Overview, Urban Governance in Bangladesh,* Dhaka Centre for Urban Studies, 199

10 Local Government in Asia and the Pacific: A Comparative Study in http://www.unescap. org/huset/lgstudy/country/bangladesh/bangladesh.html, accessed 21 August 2012.

for example, have been advocating for creating metropolitan government, modeled after Metro Manila, but the Government perceived it to be a government within government, and therefore, the proposal has not been accepted by both political regimes in Bangladesh.[11]

Local Government in the Rest of the Country

There have been several rounds of experiments with local government system in the country guided primarily by political considerations. New tiers like village level council (Gram Sarkar), Upazila Parishad (Thana or Sub-division level council) have been introduced depending on assessment of respective support bases. The present regime after coming to power in 2009 constituted a Local Government Commission which recommended the following local government bodies:

- Palli/Gram Parishad (Village Council)
- Union Parishad
- Upazila Parishad
- Zila Parishad
- Hill District Local Government.

Of these, Palli/Gram Parishad was not implemented. Through an Act of the Parliament, the present regime has scrapped the provision of Gram Sarker in April 2009.[12] Upazila Parishad was introduced by the Ershad regime in the 1980s but fell into disrepute in the 1990s despite its apparent successful experiment and popularity. Because of civil society demand, the system was revived through an act of the Parliament in 1998.[13] Further modification was introduced in the Upazila system through an Act by the present regime in 2009. The Act declared all the 463 Thanas (Police Stations) into Upazilas. Compared to the Upazila system of 1980s, two

11 See, Golam Moinuddin, " Metropolitan Government And Improvement Potentials Of Urban Basic Services Governance In Dhaka City, Bangladesh: Rhetoric Or Reality?", *Theoretical and Empirical Researches in Urban Management,* (Romania), 5(14), February 2010: 59-81.

12 See, daily *Financial Express,* (Dhaka) April 7, 2009.

13 See, A.M.M. Shawkat Ali, "Local Government, 1971-2000", in A.M. Chowdhury and Fakrul Alam (eds.), *Bangladesh: On the Threshold of the Twenty-First Century,* Dhaka: Asiatic Society of Bangladesh, 2002: 364.

new elements were introduced in 1998: (a) gender dimension, (b) the Member of Parliament (Sangshad) of the concerned constituency was made adviser to the Parishad.[14] The provision, however, did not spell out what would happen if the Upazila Parishad did not act at the dictate of the local MP. The executive power of the Upazila Parishad will be exercised by the chairman, the vice-chairman and any member or official entrusted by the Parishad. However, the provision of MP's role has been strongly resented by the civil society, in general, and the Upazila chairmen, in particular, because they suspect that although the role is advisory but it is likely to be overbearing.[15]

Zila Parishad or District Councils have traditionally been non-elected chief in the person of the Deputy Commissioner (a bureaucrat of the rank of Deputy Secretary). By an act of 2000, it was made an elected body.[16] The District has been the focal point in the administrative system of Bangladesh. The head of the district administration is known as the Deputy Commissioner (DC), a bureaucrat of the rank of Deputy Secretary.[17] The present regime in a recent move, has appointed District Administrators in different districts from amongst the political cadres. But this does not make this tier of local government an elected one. Moreover, the functions of the District Administrators remain far from clear vis-à-vis the Deputy Commissioners.

Assessment of Functioning of Local Government System

The present local government bodies in Bangladesh are subject to strong control from higher-level authorities, especially from the central government. In what follows, an assessment of the local government bodies at different tiers is made from the point of view of administrative a financial autonomy.[18]:

---

14 See, daily *The Financial Express,* April 7, 2009.

15 See, "Government not sincere to make local govts effective", *daily New Age,* 28 November 2011.

16 However, till today, the Zila Parishad remains unelected. The present regime has introduced the position of Zila Prashashak (District Administrator) which has been filled by nominated political appointees pending election.

17 Local Government in Asia and the Pacific: A Comparative Study in http://www.unescap.org/huset/lgstudy/country/bangladesh/bangladesh.html, accessed 21 August 2012.

18 Country Reports on Local Government Systems : Bangladesh, http://www.scribd.com/

Firstly, the national government retains the ultimate control over local government bodies through legislation, rules of business and other administrative leverages. It formulates detailed rules relating to conduct of elections, business, powers and duties of chairmen, assessment of taxes, preparation of budgets, making of contracts, appointment and service matters of local government employment, accounts and audits and many other important areas. Even when local governments make regulations, these are to be approved by the central government;

Secondly, the central government has the final authority in the determination of the size and boundaries of the local body's territory. The central government has the power to decide on the structure and composition of the local bodies;

Thirdly, the central government substantially controls the personnel system of local bodies, particularly the appointment of the Chief Executive Officer in City Corporations and Pourashavas as well as other officials. The central government closely supervises and controls finance, and can wield power by reducing or enhancing Grant-in-aid to local bodies, even to city authorities like Dhaka;

Fourthly, the central government asserts control and supervision over general administration of local bodies, including of large City Corporations. The central government may order an inquiry into the affairs of a local body generally or into any particular affair either on its own initiative or on an application made by any person to the government.

Fifthly, the central government has the power to dissolve a local body on charge of gross inefficiency, abuse of power, or inability to meet financial obligations, although instances of such action in Bangladesh have been rare in recent times.

Sixthly, the Government is not enthusiastic about the recommendation to transfer or devolve 26 Departments of the central government at the Upazila and Zila levels. The autonomy of urban local governments is also yet to be discussed, and was not included in the Terms of reference of the Commission set up in 1997. The recent opposition to Dhaka's proposal of forming a Metropolitan government indicates increased resistance even to

doc/26850693/Country-Reports-on-Local-Government-Systems-Bangladesh, accessed 12 August 2012.

autonomy of the largest city.

The present system of local government in Bangladesh is thus still under heavy control of the central government. There have been significant advocacy activities by civil society organizations in favour of local government strengthening. Donors are also insisting on strengthening local autonomy. However, the degree of central control even in areas traditionally falling within the purview of the local government bodies evidently has increased. Compared to 1960s and 1970s, power of local taxation for mobilization of local resources leading to autonomous self-governance has been radically curtailed.

Another development not fully captured in theories of local government is the emergence of informal governance.[19] One manifestation of informal governance in South Asia has been patron-client relations through which the entire gamut of local government hierarchies, local resource endowment and government budgetary allocations are expropriated by highly politicized clientelism. Thus, we may argue that patron-client relationship eats up whatever residual self-governing local government institutions remain in the country.

With this review of local government system in Bangladesh, we turn to the CHT Regional Council which constituted one special form of local government institution in Bangladesh. Before that, we quickly review the tribal insurgency in the CHT that created the ground for the Regional Council.

Background of the Chittagong Hill Tracts Regional Council : Tribal Insurgency

The Chittagong Hill Tracts Conflict was the political conflict and armed struggle between the Government of Bangladesh by the *Parbatya Chattagram Jana Sanghati Samiti* (United People's Party of the Chittagong Hill Tracts) and its armed wing, the *Shanti Bahini* over the issue of autonomy and the rights of the Hill tribes of the Chittagong Hill Tracts. The Shanti Bahini launched an insurgency against government forces in late 1970s, and the conflict continued for twenty years until the government

---

19 Abdur Rob Khan, "Informal Governance in South Asia: Impact on Public Policy", Paper to be presented in International Conference on *Governance and Public Policy in South and South East Asia* organized by MPPG program at North South University, Dhaka, 13-14 July, 2012

and the PCJSS signed the Chittagong Hill Tracts Peace Accord in 1997.

The conflict in the Chittagong Hill Tracts dates back to when Bangladesh was the eastern wing of Pakistan. Several factors explain the origins of the insurgency in the CHT. *Firstly*, widespread resentment occurred over the displacement of as many as 100,000 of the native peoples due to the construction of the Kaptai Hydro-electric Dam in 1962. The displaced did not receive compensation from the government and many thousands fled to India. This displacement, submergence of homesteads and agricultural lands remains a permanent scar in the psyche of the Hill peoples. The second shock came immediately after the independence of Bangladesh. After the creation of Bangladesh in 1971, representatives of the Chittagong Hill Tracts such as the Chakma politician Manabendra Narayan Larma sought autonomy and recognition of the rights of the peoples of the region. Larma and other Hill Tracts representatives protested the draft of the Constitution of Bangladesh, which did not recognise the ethnic identity and culture of the non-Bengali peoples of Bangladesh. The government policy recognised only the Bengali culture and the Bengali language and designating all citizens of Bangladesh as Bengalis. In talks with a Hill Tracts delegation led by Manabendra Narayan Larma, Bangabandhu Sheikh Mujibur Rahman insisted that the ethnic groups of the Hill Tracts adopt the Bengali identity. Consequently, Larma and others founded the Parbatya Chhatagram Jana Shanghatti Samiti (PCJSS) as a united political organisation of all native peoples and tribes in 1973. The armed wing of the PCJSS, the Shanti Bahini was organised to resist government policies. The crisis aggravated during the emergency rule of Sheikh Mujib, who had banned all political parties other than his one one party, BAKSAL and the successive military_regimes that followed after his assassination_in 1975. In 1977, the Shanti Bahini they launched their first attack on a Bangladesh Army convoy.

The third shock came when the Government of General Ziaur Rahman resettled truck loads of landless Bengalis from coastal areas in the Hill districts. The Hill people saw this as an attempt to change the demography of the CHT in favour of the plains Bengalis. Thus, the Bengali settlers became targets of the Shanti Bahini insurgency operations.

The Shanti Bahini divided its area of operations into zones and raised forces from the native people, who were formally trained. The Shanti Bahini attacked Bengali police and soldiers, government offices and personnel and the Bengali settlers in the region. The group also attacked any native believed to be opposing it and supporting the government.

Government Response with Counter-insurgency

At the outbreak of the insurgency, the Government of Bangladesh deployed the army to begin counter-insurgency operations. General Ziaur Rahman made an army general head of the Chittagong Hill Tracts Development board in order to address the socio-economic needs of the region, but the entity proved unpopular and became a source of antagonism and mistrust amongst the native people against the government. The government failed to address the long-standing issue of the displacement of people, numbering an estimated 100,000 caused by the construction of the Kaptai Dam in 1962. Displaced peoples did not receive compensation and more than 40,000 Chakma tribals had fled to India. In the 1980s, the government began settling Bengalis in the region, causing the eviction of many natives and a perceived alteration of demographics.

Negotiations with the Shanti Bahini were conducted initially by military leadership. The idea of Chakma Autonomous Hill Districts in Mizoram as a formula came in the negotiation tame in the late 1980s. Following that model, in 1989, General Hossain Mohammad Ershad passed the District Council Act created three tiers of local government councils to devolve powers and responsibilities to the representatives of the native peoples, but the councils were rejected and opposed by the PCJSS.

Peace Accord

Peace negotiations were initiated after the restoration of democracy in Bangladesh in 1991, but not much progress could be made in terms of return of the refugees from Tripura or laying down of the arms by the Shanti Bahinis, and for that matter, demilitarization of the Hill Districts. Fresh rounds of talks began in 1996 with the newly-elected Prime Minister Sheikh Hasina Wajed of the Awami League, the daughter of founding father of Bangladesh, Sheikh Mujib. The peace accord was finalised and formally signed on December 2, 1997. The agreement recognised the special status of the hill residents. The accord promised an end to hostilities, regional autonomy through devolution of powers to indigenous-controlled councils, return of occupied lands, withdrawal of most army facilities, and rehabilitation of indigenous refugees, internally displaced people and former combatants.[20]

Formation of CHT Regional Council

The Government established the Chittagong Hill Tracts Regional Council Act by an Act of 1998. The Act took three earlier Hill Districts Acts of 1988 as its basis.[21]

The 1998 CHT Regional Council Act stipulated that the Regional Council will consist of the following members:

a) Chairman;

b) Twelve Tribal Members;

c) Six Non-Tribal Members;

d) Two Tribal Female Members;

e) One Non-Tribal Female Members; and

f) Chairman of the three Hill District Councils, ex-officio;[22]:

About composition of the Regional Council, it was further stipulated that Chairman of the Council shall be elected from among tribal people. Of the tribal members,

(a) Five shall be elected from Chakma tribe;

b) Three shall be elected from Marma tribe;

c) Two shall be elected from Tripura tribe;

d) One shall be elected from the Mro and Tanchangya tribe; and

e) One shall be elected from Lushai, Bom, Pankho, Khumi, Chak

---

20 Bangladesh: Campaign for full implementation of the CHT Peace Accord to help the Jumma peoples regain control over their forests, lands, and destiny, in http://www.wrm. org.uy/bulletin/150/Bangladesh.html, accessed on August 22, 2012

21 Rangamati Hill District Council Act (Act 9 of 1988), Khagrachari Hill District Council Act (Act 10 of 1988) and Bandarban Hill District Council Act (Act 11 of 1988)

22 See, Chittagong Hill Tracts Regional Council Act, 1998 (Act 12 of 1998), Jatiya Sangsad, may 24, 1998.

and Khiang tribe.[23]

Of the non-tribal members, two shall be elected from each of the hill districts. Of the tribal female members, one shall be elected from among the Chakma tribal woman and the remaining one shall be elected from among the other tribal women. As regards the non-tribal female member, she shall be elected from among the non-tribal women of the three hill districts. The members of the council, as mentioned in sub-section 1(f), shall have the right to vote.[24]

Whether a person is non-tribal or not and if he is non-tribal, then to which community does he belong shall be determined by the Circle Chief on the basis of the certificate given to this effect by the concerned Mouza headman, or Union Council Chairman or in case of Pourashava Chairman Pourashava as the case may be, and no person shall be eligible to contest for the non-tribal member post without such a certificate given to this effect by the Circle Chief. On the other hand, whether a person is tribal or not and if he is a tribal, then to which tribe does he belong shall be decided and determined by the Circle Chief and no tribal person shall be eligible to contest for the post of chairman or tribal member without certificates given to this effect by the Circle Chief.[25]

The chairman shall have the status, and enjoy other facilities of a State Minister of the Government. The tenure of the Regional Council will be for a period of five years.

Functions of the Council

The following are the functions of the CHT Regional Council:

a) Overall supervision and coordination of all development activities under the Hill District Councils and all other matters entrusted to them. In case of disputes with the hill district councils, the decision of the Regional Council, under this Act, shall be final.

b) Supervision and coordination of the local councils including municipalities;

---

23 Ibid.

24 Ibid

25 Ibid

c) Overall supervision and coordination of the Chittagong Hill Tracts Development Board set up under the Chittagong Hill Tracts Development Board Ordinance, 1976 (LXXVII of 1976);

d) Supervision and coordination of the general administration of the hill districts, law and order and development;

e) Supervision and coordination of tribal traditions, practices etc. and social justice;

f) Issuing licenses for setting up heavy industries in hill districts in keeping with the National Industrial Policy.

g) To conduct disaster management and relief work and co-ordinating of NGO activities.

Finances of the Regional Council

The Council shall have a fund called Chittagong Hill Tracts Regional Council Fund consisting of:[26]

a) All moneys, payable from the Hill District Council Funds, fixed by the government from time to time.

b) Money or profits earned from property, if any, entrusted to and managed by the council.

c) Loans or grants received from the Government or other authorities;

d) Donations given by any organization or person;

e) Profits earned from investments of the Council's funds;

f) Any money received by the council;

g) Money received from other income sources entrusted to the Council by Government directives.

Implementation of the Accord

While in the initial years of Sheikh Hasina's first regime (1996-2001), strategic aspects of the Shanti Banhini insurgency was addressed, implementation of the accord soon began to lose momentum in such areas

---

26 Ibid.

as rehabilitation of tribal refugees in their own land, functioning of the land commission, withdrawal of temporary military camps, and most importantly, holding of elections in the Hill District councils as well as the Regional Council. Thus, the newly created local and regional bodies remain unelected. Possibly this is the most crucial lacuna of the Accord. The local people could not get the taste of local autonomy granted in the 1997 Accord and subsequent CHT Regional Council Act of 1999. In the process, wide perception gap developed between the PCJSS leadership and the Government, so much so, that at one point, the Government claimed 98 percent of the Accord has been implemented while the tribal leaders claimed that 98 percent of the Accord remains unimplemented.

However, after the present regime had come to power, a meeting of the CHT Accord Implementation Monitoring Committee was held in October 2009 to assess the progress of the implementation of the CHT Accord. Among others, amendment of CHT Land Dispute Resolution Act 2001 as per recommendation of CHT Regional Council, transfer of subjects to the three Hill District Councils (HDCs), approval of Rules of CHT Regional Council and three HDCs; setting up of separate offices for CHT Accord Implementation Monitoring Committee, CHT Land Commission and Task Force and appointment of adequate staffs for proper functioning of these offices, withdrawal of all temporary camps were discussed in the meeting.

In particular, transfer of subject to the HDCs prioritizing law and order, police (local), land and land management, secondary education, environment, youth development, local tourism etc through office order instead of the agreement between the HDC and concerned ministry were discussed.

Finally, decisions were made to set up three separate offices for the CHT Accord Implementation Monitoring Committee, CHT Land Commission and Task Force and to take effective measures for appointment of adequate staffs and providing logistic support for proper functioning of these offices.

In the meeting the issues of Land disputes and land survey were emphatically discussed. The Chairman of Land Commission emphasized for the land survey at the moment. Mr. Bir Bahadur, MP and J B Larma, President of PCJSS in particular explained that unless land disputes were resolved through the Land Commission land survey could not be arranged in CHT.

However, subsequently, the priorities of the regime seem to have changed and implementation of the Accord has again slowed down.

Perceptions of the Stakeholders

The CHT Accord of 1997 was rejected out rightly by the then Opposition, Bangladesh Nationalist Party (BNP) on the ground that it was a surrender of sovereignty to a segment of the populace through granting of special status and not allowing citizens of other parts of the country to buy lands and settle in CHT with out permission of Regional Council and local authorities. The BNP staged herbal and a long march to CHT. It evoked protests from Bengali settlers also.

Local reactions from the tribal population were also not that supportive. At least three smaller political groups in the Chittagong Hill Tracts, namely the Hill Students Council, the Hill Peoples Council and the Hill Women Federation challenged the right of the PCJSS to be the sole representative of the tribal people and sign the accord on their behalf. They also criticised the Accord because the Accord failed to address the question of constitutional recognition of the distinct identity of the Jummas. They have been demanding, autonomy with a self governing legislature, withdrawal of illegal plainsmen settlers and military camps and return of the lands to the original Jumma owners[27]

But few of these promises were fulfilled in subsequent years, particularly under the alliance government (2001-2006) of the Bangladesh Nationalist Party and Jamaat-i-Islam, which had opposed the accord, and the subsequent caretaker government. The situation was further complicated by bloody internal strife between the PCJSS and the UPDF, a Jumma political party (formed in 1998) that rejected the accord in favor of "full-autonomy" within the state of Bangladesh. Communal attacks and land grabbing continued unabated.

Recent Developments

---

27 Presentation to the Commission on Human Rights, Sub-Commission on Promotion and Protection of Human Rights, Working Group on Minorities, 10th Session, 1-5 March 2004by Leena Chakma on behalf of Ain O Shalish Kendro (ASK)

In an important development, the High Court declared that the Chittagong Hill Tracts Regional Council Act of 1998 was unconstitutional for violating the "sanctity of a unitary state", but that the CHT Peace Accord is legal.[28] The High Court bench gave the ruling on a petition challenging the peace accord. The High Court had earlier ruled that it could not consider the constitutionality of the Chittagong Hill Tracts Peace Accord. It held that the since the agreement was political in nature - "an accord between belligerents" – it could not be judicially reviewed by the court. The present government has gone on appeal and as a result, the decision and judgment was stayed by the Appellate Division of the Supreme Court pending hearing of the appeal.[29]

Secondly, the PCJSS protested the 15th Amendment of the Constitution which again complicated the nationality question by reintroducing 'Bengali' nationalism. PCJSS rejected the Fifteen Constitution (Amendment) Bill 2011 and asked the government for its revision. PCJSS leaders expressed their agitation in a large public meeting held on 8 July 2011 in Rangamati district headquarters in the CHT reiterating their demands for full implementation of the CHT Accord.[30] Mr. Larma also said that the Jumma people in the CHT are still being denied their rights. He also alleged that the withdrawal of the military camps as per the Accord was not taking place and military rule as well as Bengali settlement was continuing. He also argued that the Land Commission was intentionally kept dysfunctional.[31]

Yet in a third development, the UN Economic and Social Council in a study on implementation of the CHT Accord raised an altogether new issue, recognition of the Hill tribal people as Adivasi or indigenous people. Bangladeshi indigenous (tribal) people have been holding meetings, human chains and rallies frequently in different parts of the country, demanding constitutional recognition. They said they did not want to be termed as "tribal" groups or "small ethnic" groups but as "adivasi" (indigenous people), in line with UN conventions, to protect their cultural,

---

28 See, bdnews24.com in bdnews24.com/at/db/rah/1243h, dated April 13,2010 accessed 22 August 2012.

29 21. S. Chandrashekharan, "Bangladesh: Poor Records in implementation of CHT Peace Accord of 1997", *Paper No. 4877*, South Asia Analysis Group, 24 January, 2012.

30 See, Press Release by PCJSS, http://pcjss-cht.org/PCJSS-Consti-IP-Bengali.php, acccsscd August 222, 2012.

31 Ibid.

traditional and land rights. Suranjit Sengupta, a veteran parliamentarian and constitution expert from the ruling Awami League Party said on March 15 that the committee would recommend recognizing them (tribal people) as "small ethnic groups."[32]

In the meantime, leaders of Hill people communities reiterated their demand for constitutional recognition as "indigenous" or "adivasi" people instead of "tribal" or "small ethnic" groups, as according to them they fulfil all the United Nations' criteria to that end. The demand was made by the Bangladesh Forum for the Indigenous People, ahead of the International Day for Indigenous People. The forum leaders said the position of Bangladesh government at the United Nations Permanent Forum on Indigenous Issues (UNPFII) that there are no indigenous people in the country actually "ruined the country's image". The Foreign Minister of Bangladesh, Dipu Moni, said the constitution recognises all "ethnic minorities" and the government is pledge-bound to protect their distinct uniqueness either in hills or in the plain land. "We need to preserve and protect the uniqueness of the minorities because these distinct identities are part of the nation's beauty," she said.[33] On the other hand, the Hill people argue that they are 'indigenous' as per the ILO Convention (169), article 1 that says, "Self-identification as indigenous or tribal shall be regarded as a fundamental criterion for determining the groups to which the provisions of this Convention apply". He said Bangladesh ratified that ILO convention.[34] This issue has significantly complicated implementation of the accord.

Conclusion

There is no denying the fact that the 1997 peace accord has ensured a pause on long-standing self-determination armed conflict. However, unless the question of autonomy of CHT, which was the root cause of conflict, is resolved by implementing the peace accord and addressing the issues and challenges concerned with such implementation, it would be unrealistic to expect sustainable peace in CHT. The sooner the provisions of the accord are implemented, the quicker will be the mitigation of many of the existing

---

32 See, http://chtnewsupdate.blogspot.com/2011/05/bangladesh-indigenous-debatereaches.html accessed on August 22, 2012.

33 See, *The Daily Star,* August 5, 2011.

34 Ibid.

problems and the elimination of the causes of potential conflict. Although there was no time frame in the accord for its implementation, it is time to develop a time-bound action plan so that stagnation in implementation of the various provisions of the peace accord does not create any doubt about a lasting peace. In addition, measure should be taken to ensure constitutional recognition of CHT so that the peace accord can be immune from constitutional litigation. Care should also be taken to reach a political consensus in support of the accord at national as well as regional level before the fragility of the ongoing peace is exposed. In particular, harmony between indigenous and non-indigenous people, who are almost equal in number and almost likewise victims of government policy, is a prime condition for the congenial atmosphere that might accelerate the pace of implementation of the accord.

The Federal Debate in Sri Lanka

Rohan Edrisinha

In recent years, Sri Lanka has seriously considered the federal idea as a basis for a political solution to the island's protracted ethnic conflict. There remains, however, steadfast opposition to the federal idea among significant sections of the island's Sinhalese majority and many of these anti-federalists are now part of the Rajapakse Administration that has governed the country since 2005. The chapter seeks to discuss the federal debate in Sri Lanka placing it in historical context, critically examine the reasons why federalism has once again in recent years become so unacceptable in the island's political discourse and reaffirm the arguments in favour of a federal based solution to the island's ethnic conflict.

Federalism in the Political Discourse of the Country

Federalism has been part of Sri Lanka's political discourse for a long time. In the 1920s, the young S.W.R.D. Bandaranaike, who later formed the Sinhala nationalist Sri Lanka Freedom Party and became Ceylon's fourth post independence Prime Minister in 1956, delivered a series of lectures in Jaffna, in which he argued that a federal Ceylon would be appropriate for the island given its ethnic diversity. Interestingly in one of his lectures he suggested that the island be part of a larger federal India. Reports of the lectures indicate that there were many critics and skeptics from among the Tamil members of the audience who expressed doubts as to how a federal Ceylon would address the grievances and aspirations of Tamils leaving outside the northern peninsula.[1] In 1927, when the Donoughmore Commission was sent to Ceylon to study and recommend proposals for a new Constitution for the country, a delegation from the Kandyan National Association, submitted proposals to the Commission, calling for a federal Ceylon with a large Kandyan province in the centre of the island as part of

---

1 Edirisinha, R., Gomez, M. Thamilmaran, V.T., Welikala, A., (eds.), 2008, Power-Sharing in Sri Lanka: Constitutional and Political Documents, 1926–2008, Colombo, Centre for Policy Alternatives, p. 26

a three unit federal structure. The Kandyans were concerned that people from outside the province, non-Kandyans, were migrating to the region and that the identity of the 'Kandyan nation' would be jeopardized as a result.[2] The federal proposal did not receive support from other Ceylonese groups, including the Tamils, and was rejected by the Donoughmore Commission. It is significant therefore that the first advocates of federalism in Ceylon/ Sri Lanka were from the majority Sinhalese community and that these proposals failed to evoke a positive response from the Tamil political leadership at the time.

Even in the immediate pre-independence and post-independence period, the middle to late 1940s, the Tamil political leadership did not espouse federalism. It is possible to identify three distinct phases in Tamil political demands from this time to the present – the G.G. Ponnambalam approach of 1945–1952 of engagement at the heart of government with minority safeguards; the S.J.V. Chelvanayakam approach of 1950–1974 of federalism but with willingness to consider reasonable alternative regional autonomy options; and the more recent Velupillai Prabakaran approach, 1975–2009, of strong Tamil nationalism and secession.

In the run up to independence, two Communist Party politicians, Pieter Keuneman and A. Vaitialingam, proposed that a two nation federal constitution be considered for Ceylon. The proposal received little support. The preferred option of the main Tamil political party, the All Ceylon Tamil Congress, ACTC, and its leader, G.G. Ponnambalam Snr., was to share power at the centre and ensure that minority rights were protected rather than a demand for decentralization of power. Ponnambalam's controversial 50– 50 proposal was that the legislature should have 50 per cent of the seats for Sinhalese with the other half reserved for all minorities, the Tamils, Muslims, Burghers, and other minority groups. The somewhat simplistic rationale for the proposal was that it would be unlikely that such a constituted legislature would enact legislation that was discriminatory against minorities. Ponnambalam and the ACTC also decided to accept a Cabinet portfolio in the first post independence Cabinet of Ministers, thereby facilitating participation at the centre of government, which in turn, he believed, would ensure that Tamil concerns and aspirations could be raised and addressed right at the heart of where power was located.

---

2 Roberts, M. 'Problems of Collective Identity in a Multi-Ethnic Society: Sectional Nationalism vs. Ceylonese Nationalism', 1900–1940 in Sri Lanka, Collective Identities Revisited.

It was when the Ponnambalam approach was perceived to have failed that Tamil support moved to the Chelvanayakam approach which stressed the importance of decentralization and autonomy in Tamil majority areas of the country. Chelvanayakam broke away from the ACTC and formed the Federal Party or Ilankai Tamil Arasu Kachchi or Tamil State party (as it was known in Tamil fuelling fears that it was really committed to secession) and for the first time the Tamil political leadership espoused federalism as its basic political demand. Chelvanayakam was a committed Gandhian who believed in peaceful, non-violent, democratic means for the pursuit of federalism. He was also willing to consider reasonable alternatives to federalism as he did in 1957 and 1965 when he entered into two well known agreements with Prime Ministers of Ceylon, S.W.R.D. Bandaranaike in the Bandaranaike-Chelvanayakam Pact of 1957 and Dudley Senanayake, the so-called 'Dudley-Chelva Pact' of 1965. Both these agreements envisaged decentralization of power to the north and the east, with the possibility of northern and eastern region together working. The intention was to introduce these reforms through legislation rather than by a constitutional amendment. The agreements, therefore, fell short of basic features of federalism but on both occasions, opposition from both within the ruling coalition governments and from outside, forced both Prime Ministers to withdraw their support from the agreements. It must be noted that during the 1950s and 60s, Tamil frustrations continued on other issues as well. Laws dealing with citizenship and language that were discriminatory against the Tamils were enacted and legal challenges to such initiatives on the basis that they violated the much touted minority protection provision of the Constitution, Section 29, failed due to the legalistic and positivist approach of the judiciary, and therefore, in general, there was growing frustration at the rise of Sinhalese majoritarianism in addition to the failure of Ceylonese governments to respond positively to demands for regional autonomy. Tamil youth and nationalist elements began to become impatient with the Chelvanayakam approach, which they argued, had failed to deliver positive results.

This discontent became evident at the time of the General Election of 1970. A number of independent Tamil candidates contested in electorates in the north on a platform of secession and a stronger brand of Tamil nationalism than that advocated by the Federal Party. The response of the Federal Party to its challengers was noteworthy. Its manifesto declared,

The Tamil-speaking people of Ceylon also believe that the Federal-type of Constitution that would enable them to look after their own affairs alone would safeguard them from total extinction. Only under such a Constitution could the Tamil speaking people of this country live in dignity and with our birthright to independence as equals with our Sinhala brethren.

Significantly, the manifesto included a categorical repudiation of separation:

It is our firm conviction that division of the country in any form would be beneficial neither to the country nor the Tamil speaking people. Hence we appeal to the Tamil speaking people not to lend their support to any political movement that advocates the bifurcation of the country. The candidates who adopted a pro-secessionist line were heavily defeated and the Federal Party swept the polls in the north and the east.

Sri Lanka's Republican Constitutions

The parliamentary elections of 1970 not only resulted in the Federal Party sweeping the polls in Tamil majority areas, but it also gave a sweeping victory to the United Front, a coalition of the Sinhala nationalist Sri Lanka Freedom Party and the Marxist parties who till this time had little opportunity to participate in government. The coalition obtained a two-third majority in Parliament and decided to initiate a process of constitutional reform to replace the Soulbury Constitution that was introduced before independence and served as the country's independence Constitution since 1948. A Constituent Assembly consisting of all members of the House of Representatives elected at the 1970 elections was convened and assigned the responsibility of drafting and adopting a new Constitution. The fact that the United Front government possessed a clear majority in the Assembly and a two-thirds majority in Parliament made it arrogant and unwilling to accommodate opposition proposals. The Minister of Constitutional Affairs, veteran Trotskyist, Colvin R. de Silva, initiated proposals in the form of basic resolutions that were debated and then voted upon. He proposed in Basic Resolution No. 2 that the new constitution should include a provision expressly declaring that 'Sri Lanka is a unitary state.' The Soulbury Constitution, though clearly unitary in character contained no such express label or self description.

Dr Colvin R. de Silva stated somewhat ambiguously that 'from the time that we can remember' Sri Lanka had been a unitary state.[3] He defended the introduction of the unitary label on the grounds that it was essential for the well being of the country as a whole. The main criticism of the proposal was made by V. Dharmalingam, the Federal Party M.P. for Uduvil. He highlighted the importance of a constitution being an agreement of all the people of the country and warned against the Sinhala people imposing a constitution on the Tamil people. He then presented the classic defence of a federal constitution; that it was more appropriate for a multi-ethnic, plural society. Dharmalingam argued that the Federal Party desired the establishment of a federal state in Ceylon, not to divide Ceylon, but to achieve unity in diversity. He predicted that ultimately Ceylon would have to be a federal state.[4]

Several Marxist MPs in the government however argued that a strong, centralized political framework was essential for the establishment of socialism where the means of production, distribution and exchange belonged to the people of those countries. Ratne Deshapriya Senanayake declared that it was only under a unitary state that a socialist national development plan could be implemented effectively. While there were defenders of the unitary postulate for Sinhalese nationalist reasons, it is interesting to note the defence for socialist reasons.

The unitary postulate was reinforced by Section 45 (1) of the Constitution which stated that:

> *The National State Assembly may not abdicate, delegate or in any manner alienate its legislative power, nor may it set up an authority with any legislative power other than the power to make subordinate laws.*

The First Republican Constitution of 1972 made things worse in terms of several other substantive constitutional provisions it introduced. Not only did it abolish many of the minority safeguards, including Section 29 of the Soulbury Constitution, but it also entrenched majoritarianism in the supreme law of the land. The secular character of the state was severely undermined by the provision that gave Buddhism the foremost place. The language of the majority, Sinhalese, was made the sole official language.

---

3 Constituent Assembly Debates, 1971, Vol. I, 16th March 1971.

4 Ibid. at column 386

As one looks back at the evolution of Sri Lanka's ethnic conflict, one is almost shocked by the short-sighted, populist motivations to the introduction of these features. Indeed the decision to insert the unitary label into the First Republican Constitution seems almost perverse in that it was a direct affront to Tamil aspirations at the time. The introduction of the Constitution of 1972 was, therefore, a major landmark in the process of national disintegration.

The Second Republican Constitution of 1978 suffered from the same basic defect of the previous Constitution; a concentration of power in one institution. The Executive Presidential system vested enormous power in a single institution/individual. A.J. Wilson's description of the Constitution as Gaullist in character[5] is misleading as the Sri Lankan President enjoys many powers that his/her French counterpart does not. The President's complete immunity from legal proceedings, the unilateral power to dissolve Parliament, the ability to assign to himself/herself ministerial portfolios and the power to legislate by emergency regulation provide the office with great powers. Such an over mighty executive coupled with a devalued Parliament consisting of ambassadors of parties, rather than representatives of the People, and the fact that most of the parties practice very little intra-party democracy combine to create a centralized political structure consisting of centralized political forces. The article declaring Sri Lanka to be a unitary state was reproduced as were the articles prohibiting the alienation of legislative power from the Parliament of Sri Lanka. The unitary principle was made even more secure as it was part of a series of articles that were granted special protection, the so-called entrenched articles, the amendment of which required, in addition to the usual two-thirds majority affirmative vote in Parliament, the approval of the People at a Referendum.

It was the fact that the unitary postulate was entrenched that posed a particular challenge for President Jayewardene and his government when they sought to introduce the Thirteenth Amendment to the Constitution. Though the Jayewardene Government had toyed with the idea of decentralization or devolution of power in the early 1980s, it was the pressure on the Government particularly after the anti-Tamil violence of July 1983 from the Indian Government that prompted Jayewardene

---

5   Wilson, A.J., 1978, The Gaullist System in Asia: The Constitution of Sri Lanka, Macmillan, 1980.

to introduce constitutional reforms which violated the whole ethos of his Constitution and also his own political instincts. In 1987, the Indian Government virtually forced Jayewardene into signing the Indo-Lanka Accord, under which the Sri Lankan government undertook to introduce a constitutional amendment providing for devolution to provinces. A system of devolution of power was thus sought to be incorporated into a Constitution which had been designed to centralize power. The last thing the Jayewardene Government wanted in 1987 was to have a referendum on such a sensitive political issue. His government was unpopular after Jayewardene's controversial, and in my view, unconstitutional, extension of the life of Parliament by the Referendum of 1982 and his government's conduct during the tragedy of July 1983, even among its natural constituencies.

The introduction of the Thirteenth Amendment was challenged by an array of petitioners, including the Leader of the Opposition, Sirimavo Bandaranaike, before the Sri Lankan Supreme Court.[6] The basis of the challenge was that since the scheme of devolution to provincial councils envisaged by the amendment violated Article 2 of the Constitution that declared that 'Sri Lanka is a unitary state' the amendment had to be approved at a Referendum in addition to being passed with a two-thirds majority vote in Parliament. Some petitioners even invoked the Indian Basic Structure doctrine to suggest that the 'unitary principle' and the prohibition on any alienation of legislative power in Article 76 of the Constitution, were basic features of the Constitution and were therefore unalterable. The Chief Justice, wisely, decided not to choose a panel of judges who would sit with him to consider the constitutional challenge, but instructed all the judges of the Supreme Court to hear the case, a rare occurrence in Sri Lanka.[7] It is widely accepted that there was powerful pressure applied on the Court by the government in this high profile case that involved nearly all the island's legal luminaries in the Bar. Chief Justice Sharvananda and four judges finally held that the amendment did not violate the unitary character of the Constitution and therefore did not require a referendum for adoption. The second most senior judge, Justice

---

6 The Supreme Court functions as a Constitutional Court and is given the responsibility of deciding whether a Constitutional amendment may be passed by a two-thirds majority vote in Parliament or whether in addition to such a majority, it requires the approval of the People at a Referendum.

7 See In Re the thirteenth Amendment to the Constitution, 1987, 2 SLR 312.

Wanasundera and three of his colleagues held that it did and therefore required a referendum. The majority view highlighted the numerous ways in which the centre retained effective control despite the introduction of a second tier of government, while the minority view focused on the statute making powers of the newly established councils. The two positions differed ultimately on the balance of power in the new scheme with the minority deciding that the tilt in favour of the provinces was sufficient to conclude that the country was no longer unitary.

Perhaps because the Thirteenth Amendment sought to introduce devolution within the framework of a unitary state the devolution was not substantial and secure. It provided for a veneer of devolution while retaining vast powers with the centre. The Amendment, ultimately, failed to grant complete control over any subject to a Provincial Council. It was also easy for the centre to retake power; this could, in the areas of health and education, for example, even be done by a Central Government Ministerial directive. There was also no clear division of power between the central government and the Provincial Councils. The Thirteenth Amendment contained three lists spelling out the subjects devolved to the Provincial Councils (List I), the subjects retained by the centre in the Reserved List (List II) and also a Concurrent List (List III). Ultimately all the subjects specified in the Concurrent List, were under the control of Parliament. Furthermore the drafting style of the lists demonstrated that the subjects and functions under the Reserved List were drafted in a manner that was wide and inclusive, whereas the Provincial List was drafted in a manner that was narrow and limiting.

A major flaw in the Thirteenth Amendment to the Constitution was that the first phrase in the Reserved List completely undermined powers apparently devolved under the Provincial Councils List. It provided for 'National Policy on all Subjects and Functions' (even those subjects in the Provincial and Concurrent Lists) to be determined by the central Parliament. A clear example of how devolution of power was undermined by the use of this provision was the National Transport Commission Bill which was presented in Parliament by the Minister of Transport and Highways on 23rd July 1991. The preamble of the Bill began with the words 'Whereas it is the national policy of the Government of Sri Lanka ...'. Thus the central Parliament successfully encroached into the Provincial sphere by cloaking itself with the protection of the national policy rubric in the Reserved List.

Under the Thirteenth Amendment and the Provincial Councils Act,

- The Central Parliament and Provincial Councils were not coordinate sovereignties;

- There was no clear division of power between the centre and the provinces;

- The powers of Provincial Councils could be reduced or abolished by the central government acting unilaterally;

- There was no subject over whom a Provincial Council can claim to exercise exclusive competence or jurisdiction;

- Central government institutions either directly or indirectly exercised considerable control over Provincial Councils.

The fact that the Thirteenth Amendment was incorporated into a Constitution that provided for a centralized political structure with an over mighty Executive President contributed to the retention of power at the centre and the undermining of effective devolution of power.

Furthermore a number of other constitutional features, many of which are found in federal countries including India, are conspicuously absent in the Sri Lankan Constitution. In Sri Lanka, unlike in India, there is a constitutional prohibition on judicial review of legislation, there is no independent public service and there is no mechanism like the Rajya Sabha, to facilitate provincial representation at the centre. The absence of comprehensive judicial review of legislation combined with the wide immunity given to the President, preventing the President from being made a party to legal proceedings for acts or omissions, permitted important sections of the Thirteenth Amendment dealing with police powers and land to be non-implemented since the introduction of the amendment in 1987 to date.

It was, therefore, not surprising that Tamil political parties called for 'substantial devolution of power' totally rejecting the existing constitutional framework. The problem was not confined to 'a lack of political will to devolve power' alone. The constitutional provisions themselves were fundamentally flawed. They permit the centre both to retain power and also undermine devolved powers so easily, that it effectively precludes substantial devolution of power.

Post 13th Amendment Constitutional Developments

There were several initiatives since 1988 to develop a political solution to the ethnic conflict. It is important to note that they all proceeded on the assumption that the system of devolution of power introduced by the Thirteenth Amendment was inadequate, had failed to respond to Tamil grievances and aspirations and failed to introduce secure and effective devolution of power. In a significant change of policy, the manifesto of the Democratic People's Alliance of Sirimavo Bandaranaike for the 1988 Presidential election campaign included proposals for enhanced devolution of power and the reintroduction of the main minority safeguard at the time of independence, Section 29 (2), a proposal of symbolic significance to reach out to the Tamil community.

The All Party Conference convened by President Premadasa, (who had defeated Ms. Babdara Naike at the 1988 Presidential election) in the early 1990s discussed options for enhanced devolution of power and a conditional merger of the northern and eastern provinces to protect Muslim interests while addressing Tamil aspirations for the two provinces to unite.

G.G. (Kumar) Ponnambalam Jnr. of the All Ceylon Tamil Congress and M.H.M Ashraff, the leader of the Sri Lanka Muslim Congress played key roles in developing these options and persuading Tamil and Muslim political leaders of the need for accommodation on the part of Tamil and Muslim parties. This was followed by the appointment of the Mangala Moonesinghe Parliamentary Select Committee where Mangala Moonesinghe's perseverance and commitment contributed to a report that demonstrated a recognition of the limitations of the Thirteenth Amendment and recommended a political solution on the lines of Indian style federalism.[8]

The constitutional reform project of the Chandrika Kumaratunga Administration from 1995–2000 was clearly an attempt to remove the authoritarian features of the Second Republican Constitution and also introduce substantial devolution of power that specifically overcame the inherent weaknesses of the Thirteenth Amendment. Removing the

---

8 Loganathan, K. 1996, Sri Lanka, Lost Opportunities-Past Attempts at Resolving Ethnic Conflict, CEPRA, Colombo, University of Colombo, p. 167, p. 228.

pro-central bias in the formulation of the lists of subjects and functions, abolishing the concurrent list, ensuring clarity with respect to the division of powers, enhancing the revenue raising powers of the proposed regional councils, and removing the unitary label from the constitution thereby recognizing the anomaly in seeking to devolve substantial power within the confines of a unitary constitutional framework. Constitutional scholar and moderate TNA M.P. Neelan Tiruchelvam, played a key role in sensitizing those who played a leadership role in the Government and the Ministry of Constitutional Affairs on Tamil political aspirations and the limitations of the Thirteenth Amendment in addressing such aspirations.

The constitutional reform initiative failed due to the irresponsible response of the opposition United National Party to the initiative. Ultimately President Kumaratunga's reluctance to abolish the Executive Presidency at the time of adoption of the new Constitution provided the UNP with the excuse it was looking for to torpedo the new constitution. In fairness to the UNP, however, it did not oppose the provisions in the draft Constitution on devolution of power, which were a significant advance on the Thirteenth Amendment. There was more opposition to these provisions from among hawks within the ruling party, including Ministers Mahinda Rajapakse and Ratnasiri Wickremanayake.

The initiative that went furthest in responding positively to Tamil nationalist demands was that which took place during the co-habitation government of President Kumaratunga and Prime Minister Ranil Wickremasinghe between 2002 and 2003. President Kumaratunga compelled to share power with a UNP dominated Cabinet of Ministers and Parliament, took a back seat and permitted Wickremasinghe to sign a cessation of hostilities agreement in February 2002 and embark upon a Norwegian facilitated series of negotiations with the Liberation Tigers of Tamil Eelam (LTTE). The Forum of Federations, an Ottawa based international organization, was accepted by both the Government and the LTTE as an Advisor to the process rather than exclusively to either party. The Forum's President, former Ontario premier, Bob Rae and University of Toronto, Department of Political Science, David Cameron, represented the Forum at the negotiations. The most significant accomplishment of the negotiation process in terms of progress on achieving a political solution was at the round of talks held in Oslo in December 2002, when the so-called Oslo agreement was reached. The Government's chief negotiator, G.L. Peiris, the Minister of Constitutional Affairs during the Kumaratunga constitutional reform initiative who had subsequently joined Wickremasinghe's UNP, acknowledged that the Forum's contribution to the agreement was significant.

The promise of the Oslo agreement cannot be understood without taking into consideration the Thimpu Principles of 1985, a set of four principles enunciated by all Tamil political groups that participated, albeit as reluctant negotiators, in an Indian sponsored conference in 1985 in Thimpu, Bhutan. The Tamil parties, including the TULF and the LTTE, expressed their basic demands which subsequently evolved into a widely held consensus set of principles among Tamil political groups.

The four cardinal principles placed before the Sri Lanka Government delegation at the Thimpu talks by the six Tamil organizations represented there (the TULF, LTTE, EPRLF, EROS, PLOTE and TELO) were:

- Recognition of the Tamils of Sri Lanka as a distinct nationality;

- Recognition of an identified Tamil homeland and the guarantee of its territorial integrity;

- Based on the above, recognition of the inalienable right of self-determination of the Tamil nation;

- Recognition of the right to full citizenship and other fundamental democratic rights of all Tamils, who look upon the island as their country.

The first three principles were rejected by the Government delegation on the grounds that they necessarily implied the destruction of a united Sri Lanka. The leader of the delegation, H.W. Jayewardene said,

> ... *If the first three principles are to be taken at their face value and given their accepted legal meaning, they are wholly unacceptable to the Government. They must be rejected for the reason that they constitute a negation of the sovereignty and territorial integrity of Sri Lanka, they are detrimental to a united Sri Lanka and are inimical to the interests of the several communities, ethnic and religious in our country.*[9]

---

9 Ibid. at pp 105.

Mr Jayewardene assumed that they had an accepted legal meaning and that they would necessarily violate the sovereignty and unity of the country.

The problem with the Thimpu Principles, which was probably their attraction for the LTTE and some Tamil nationalist groups, was their ambiguity. To many, including H.W. Jayewardene's delegation that included many conservative, hawkish Sinhalese lawyers, and also to Tamil 'strong nationalists', the Thimpu Principles stood for a separate, independent nation-state. However, as those familiar with the Canadian experience will understand, the Thimpu Principles could also be interpreted differently and accommodated within an existing nation state. At the time however and in subsequent years the ambiguity of the Thimpu Principles was useful to the Tamil nationalist project and there was no desire to clarify their meaning or spell out what they would mean in terms of constitutional architecture. This posed difficulties particularly for the Sinhalese majority and the Muslims in the eastern province who feared that any form of accommodation of the Thimpu principles would lead to secession.

The significance of the Oslo statement of December 2002 was that it did precisely that. The ambiguity of the principles that had assumed greater significance to Tamil nationalists in later years was clarified to a considerable extent. The LTTE and the Government of Sri Lanka agreed to explore a federal solution based on the principles of internal self determination, in areas of historical habitation of the Tamil people, within a united Sri Lanka and that the solution should be acceptable to all communities, a clear indication that the Muslim community should be engaged in developing the political solution. The references to internal self determination and a united Sri Lanka were crucial in allaying the consistent and perennial fear of the Sinhalese, that federalism was a stepping stone to secession. For the Government of Sri Lanka responding positively to the federal idea and internal self determination was not too difficult given the groundwork of the constitution reform project of 1995– 2000 where the limitations of the unitary state and the Thirteenth Amendment had been widely discussed and debated in the public arena.

While the initiative to introduce a new constitution might have failed, the public awareness and education campaigns both of the government and civil society certainly had an impact. People were more sensitized to the challenges of constitutional design for a plural society and conflict resolution, the need for a political solution to a problem that was essentially political in nature, and the inadequacy of a solely militarist response.

The promise of the Oslo agreement was not without problems. Soon afterwards there were statements from the LTTE that raised doubts about its commitment to the Oslo formulation; the negotiations became more difficult with both sides accusing the other of violating the cessation of hostilities agreement; the conduct of the LTTE in continuing to silence alternative voices within the Tamil community raised serious doubts as to the LTTE's commitment to pluralism, human rights, democracy and power sharing, values inextricably linked to the federal idea. The negotiations broke down just before they were to deal with a human rights memorandum of understanding a major lacuna in the agreements and negotiations up to that point and also the road map to implement the Oslo agreement.

After the negotiations resumed due to considerable international pressure the LTTE insisted that the issue of interim arrangements be the major focus and this culminated in the LTTE releasing a set of proposals for an Interim Self Governing Authority in October 2003.[10] The proposals were maximalist in nature and provoked an outcry among Sinhalese opponents of devolution of power and the Muslims in the east. While the most vociferous critics of the proposals were conservative Sinhalese lawyers committed to Sinhalese majoritarianism and the preservation of the unitary state, the proposals were also amenable to a powerful critique from a constitutionalist and federalist perspective.

The ISGA proposals were entirely about self rule with no mention at all about shared rule. The proposals were extremely weak with respect to basic constitutional principles of the rule of law, separation of powers and protection of the rights of minorities. Proposals that went far beyond powers exercised by regions in federal countries to give the ISGA control of the marine and offshore resources of the adjacent seas and control access to them were cited by critics of the negotiation process to raise doubts about both the bona fides of the LTTE and also its commitment to a federal solution. It was ironic, but not surprising, that the dominant Tamil nationalist group which for years had campaigned against the unitary, majoritarian constitutional framework of Sri Lanka when given its first

10 The Proposals by the LTTE on behalf of the Tamil People for an agreement to establish an Interim Self-Governing Authority for the North-East of the Island of Sri Lanka.

opportunity to produce constitutional proposals of its own for the north east region, produced proposals that would have resulted in a unitarist, centralized, majoritarian north east with woefully inadequate human rights and minority rights protection mechanisms. Another negative aspect of the ISGA proposals was that it suggested that the LTTE was contemplating a two-nation confederal model that international experience demonstrates is inherently unstable and conducive to disintergration, rather than a more conventional or even asymmetrical federal arrangement designed to promote unity in diversity.

The perception that the LTTE had got the better of the Government in the negotiation process in the Kumaratunga-Wickremesinghe co-habitation period, that the LTTE was not really interested in a federal type solution within a united Sri Lanka, and that they therefore, could not be trusted, was widespread at the time of the Presidential election of November 2005.

This, combined with dislike for Wickremesinghe's economic policies, provided candidate Rajapakse a platform for an effective challenge in the election. Rajapakse realizing that President Kumaratunga's support for him was lukewarm and that she controlled their party's machinery, depended for organizational support on two small Sinhalese nationalist parties the JVP and the JHU and they in turn extracted their pounds of flesh by influencing considerably the candidate's election manifesto, Mahinda Chinthanaya. The manifesto and campaign rhetoric was decidedly hawkish, unashamedly Sinhala nationalist in tone and contained a promise to preserve the unitary status of the island's constitution. The final nail in the coffin was however when the LTTE called for and forcibly implemented a boycott of the presidential elections in the north thereby depriving Wickremesinghe of a large number of Tamil votes. The LTTE helped to ensure Rajapakse's victory at the election and raised a host of new doubts about its commitment to a negotiated political settlement.

The Rajapakse Administration 2005–2009

The Rajapakse administration with the JHU and JVP in positions of influence, adopted a different approach to the ethnic conflict. Hawks were appointed to key positions, attempts to recommence negotiations failed and soon it became evident that the military response was the preferred option of the new regime. However due to pressure from more liberal elements within the government and international opinion, President

Rajapakse convened an All Party Representative Committee under the chairmanship of Trotskyist Minister Tissa Vitharna, who courageously defended the devolution proposals of the 1995–2000 era. The APRC was supposed to develop a 'southern consensus' with respect to constitutional/ political proposals that could form the basis for a negotiated political settlement. Vitharana proposed that a panel of experts be appointed to help the political parties and given the wide range of views within the government on responses to the ethnic conflict let alone devolution of power, was happy to let the panel of experts take the lead in submitting proposals. At the inaugural joint meeting of the APRC and the Panel of Experts on 11th July 2006, President Rajapakse urged the members to approach their task with a sense of urgency. He stated, "It is imperative that the process moves speedily and effectively. After more than two decades of a protracted, cruel and violent conflict, the country cannot wait any longer to usher in a just and sustainable peace for all peoples of Sri Lanka."

He added some advice also on the substantive issues involved: "I would urge that your proposals be creative and imaginative … . The role of the APRC and as well as its panel of experts is to fashion creative options." Notwithstanding these sentiments at the launch of the process, the developments since then have been anything but speedy, effective or the output from the process creative in terms of substance.

The panel of experts divided into two, early in its deliberations. Many members who were involved in the 1995–2000 process, representatives from the minority communities and officials from the government worked together and produced a set of proposals (the Majority report) similar to the basic framework of the draft Constitution of 2000. A minority of the panel consisting of several well known critics of devolution presented an interesting report that highlighted the limitations of devolution of power.

Minister Vitharana spent the latter half of 2007, trying to synthesize the two reports. When the focus shifted back from the panel of experts to the political party representatives in the APRC, Vitharana found it difficult to manage the JHU and JVP who had strong anti-devolution views and also direct access to the Presidential Secretariat.

In January 2008, in an effort to break the deadlock and lack of progress, the idea of an interim set of proposals of the APRC, based on the

13th Amendment to the Constitution was mooted by Vitharana and other pragmatists within the government. It was thought that since this would not involve legislative or constitutional reform but rather a combination of administrative actions, this would be easier to implement. At the outset it was clear that the advocates of this strategy of full implementation of the Thirteenth Amendment to the Constitution, were those who were aware of the inherent weaknesses of the amendment, the use of the national policy rubric to impose the centre's will on provincial competencies, the way in which the concurrent list subjects and functions were dominated by the centre, the non-implementation of the provisions devolving police and land powers, the tendency to bestow national status on schools and hospitals and thereby bring them under central governmental control and other strategies to undermine the Thirteenth Amendment. There was speculation in the media about a ten page document that addressed some of these issues and sought to ensure that in fact the Thirteenth Amendment was fully implemented in letter and spirit. But during the next week it became clear that there was stout resistance even to this within the APRC and among anti-devolution groups close to the President. What finally emerged was a very bare, basic and inadequate two page document with the significant change in the title – 'Action to be taken by the President to fully implement relevant provisions of the Constitution.' There was strong evidence to suggest that the JVP and the JHU had a hand in producing this truncated version of earlier drafts that was thereupon given to Minister Vitharana on the directions of the President, which in turn, was dutifully presented by Vitharana himself to the President as the APRC interim proposals.

The two page document was embarrassingly vague and threadbare. It included statements that the government should try to give the provinces more power and money and a proposal that a law should be enacted to ensure that constitutional provisions on language be implemented! There was no reference to the provisions of the Thirteenth Amendment that had not been implemented for 20 years, and indeed by promising to implement relevant rather than all provisions of the Thirteenth Amendment, the Rajapakse Government's determination to continue that practice became crystal clear. Therefore, what was ultimately proposed in the two page set of interim proposals was a continuation of the status quo with the non-implementation of significant parts of the Thirteenth Amendment – in short, Thirteenth Amendment minus. What was a little less startling than the two page memorandum itself was the statement of the Indian High Commissioner in Sri Lanka on the release of the document, that it was a positive first step. Twenty years after the introduction of the Thirteenth Amendment, after several initiatives that commenced on the assumption that the Thirteenth Amendment was inadequate, and ten years after the SLFP, UNP and the traditional left parties had explored constitutional options that went far beyond the amendment, a Thirteenth Amendment minus proposal is seriously proposed as an interim proposal for a resolution of the island's ethnic conflict.

The remainder of 2008 has basically focused on the war and the military defeat of the LTTE. President Rajapakse affirmed his belief in a political solution to the ethnic conflict when he addressed the United Nations General Assembly and when he hosted the SAARC summit. However, his discourse was very different when he spoke in the Sinhala language to the majority community of the country, where the focus was on defeating terrorism, the LTTE, and celebrating the military success of the armed forces.

Conclusion

Political leaders and those who do not wish to antagonize the wielders of power do not discuss or refer to federalism or the federal idea any more. Even the more politically acceptable phrase, power sharing, is hardly mentioned. A Select Committee of Parliament appointed in 2006 to investigate NGOs to ascertain whether they had engaged in activities prejudicial to national sovereignty has rebuked several NGOs that were at the forefront of the campaign for a federal or power sharing based political solution to the island's ethnic conflict, suggesting that its leaders were anti-national traitors. Constitutional reform for conflict resolution has moved backwards rather than forwards in the past three years. The military success of the Sri Lankan armed forces and the policies and mindsets of those who wield power at the moment, indicate that it is extremely unlikely that any meaningful proposals to enhance the devolution of power on federal lines will emerge in the foreseeable future. Today with the wisdom of hindsight it seems that the Oslo agreement of 2002 in the context of a Kumaratunga/Wickremasinghe co-habitation government and the post 1995–2000 constitution reform project might have been the best opportunity for a federal and united Sri Lanka and durable peace and reconciliation.

However, the LTTE's strong nationalism, unwillingness to embrace values of democracy, human rights and pluralism, and its intransigence as revealed in its contra-federal ISGA proposals, it is clear, have also contributed to the retrogressive developments in the struggle to resolve the island's protracted ethnic conflict. It also created grave doubts in the minds of the Sinhalese, the Muslims and the members of the international community about the group's willingness to abandon succession and accept a federal type of political structure.

The military defeat of the LTTE in May 2009 means that the military imperative for negotiations to achieve a political solution to the island's ethnic conflict no longer exists. Though Sri Lanka may have entered a post-war period, it has not yet entered a post-conflict period as the underlying causes of the conflict remain. There remains the need, therefore, for far reaching constitutional and political reform that should include substantial devolution of powers and possibly a federal constitution. Unfortunately, the Rajapakse Government, has done little to pressure such a path of constitutional and political reform.

References

Abeysekera, C., et al. (eds.), 1998, Unitarism, Devolution and Majoritarian Elitism: A response to the Interim Report of the Sinhala Commission, Colombo, Social Scientists Association.

Amaratunga, C. (ed.), 1988, Ideas for Constitutional Reform, Colombo, Council for Liberal Democracy.

Coomaraswamy, R., 1996, Ideology and the Constitution: Essays on Constitutional Jurisprudence, Colombo, ICES.

de Silva, K.M. (ed.), 1977, Sri Lanka: A Survey, London, C. Hurst and Co.

de Silva, K.M., 1986, Managing Ethnic Tensions in Multi-Ethnic Societies: Sri Lanka, 1880–1985, Lanham: University Press of America.

de Silva, K.M. & Pieris, G.H (eds.), 2000, Pursuit of Peace in Sri Lanka: Past Failures and Future Prospects, Kandy, ICES.

Edirisinha, R., & Welikala, A., (eds.), 2008, Essays on Fedaralism in Sri

Lanka, Colombo, CPA

Edirisinha, R., Welikala, A., Gomez, M, Thamilmaran V.T., (eds.), 2009, Power Sharing in Sri Lanka: Constitutional and Political Documents 1926–2008, Colombo Centre for Policy Alternatives and Berghof Foundation for Peace Support, Berlin.

Ghai. Y., (ed.), 2000, Autonomy and Ethnicity: Negotiating Claims in Multi-ethnic States, Cambridge: Cambridge University Press.

Gosh, P.S., 2003, Ethnicity versus Nationalism: The Devolution Discourse in Sri Lanka, New Delhi Sage.

Gunasekera, S.L., 1996, Tigers, 'Moderates' and Pandora's Package, Colombo, Multi Packs (Ceylon) Limited.

Hoole, R., Somasundaram, D., K., & Thirangama, R., 1990, The Broken Palmyra: The Tamil crisis in Sri Lanka – An Inside Account, Claremont-Sri Lanka Studies Institute.

Little, D., 1994, Sri Lanka: The Invention of Enmity, Washington DC, United States Institute of Peace.

Loganathan, K., 1996, Sri Lanka: Lost Opportunities, Past Attempts at Resolving Ethnic Conflict, Colombo, CEPRA, University of Colombo.

Tambiah, S.J., 1986, Sri Lanka: Ethnic Fratricide and the Dismantling of Democracy, Chicago, The University of Chicago Press.

Uyangoda, J. and Perera, M. (eds.), 2003, Sri Lanka's Peace Process 2002: Critical Perspectives, Colombo, Social Scientists' Association.

Wilson, A.J., 1994, S.J.V Chelvanayakam and the Crisis of Sri Lankan Tamil Nationalism, 1947–1977, Colombo, Lake House.

Federalism Discourse in Nepal
An Appraisal

Krishna P. Khanal

After four years of the exercise, the Constituent Assembly (CA) of Nepal rather witnessed a tragic end without delivering the much promised constitution for the newly declared 'Federal Republic'. Obviously, federalism was one of the main issues in which political parties could not reconcile the contesting claims by various ethno-regional groups as well as their own differing perceptions and positions on it. Hence the Assembly was allowed to end its tenure in the pretext of Supreme Court ruling that it could no longer be extended beyond 27th may 2012.[1] How the stalled politics would unfold and the country once again resumes the constitution making process is yet to be seen. The street which used to be mostly very hot for or against the federal issues is now calm and quite. Though the federal agenda of the new constitution for the time being seems to be in shadow but cannot be ruled out for ever. Because the issue has been deeply entrenched in Nepali politics and therefore, is sure to come up again soon the constitution making process is resumed.

Federalism had been the highly proclaimed agenda of most political parties and especially for ethno-regional forces but equally disputed particularly in its design ever since the country elected CA in April 2008. Though most of the political parties who had won seats in CA elections,[2]

---

1   The Interim Constitution, 2007 originally provided that CA had two years term counting form its first meeting which was extended to four year term via amending the Interim Constitution four times. Each amendment was challenged in Supreme Court of Nepal. The Court in its last decision delivered on 25 November 2011 had stated that the term of the assembly could not be extended beyond six months which would end by 27th May 2012. The court had further stated that if CA could not accomplish its constitution making task by then it might chose new election, referendum or any other appropriate measure.

2   If we go by the election manifestos of political parties having able to win CA seats, with the exception of Rashtriya Jana Morcha, which had only four seats in an Assembly of 601-members, all had, at least in principle, explicitly mentioned that they would frame

principally agreed to federalism they fundamentally differed in its basic design, names and number of the provinces, etc. which obviously were the entry point to federal state. Ever since the CA thematic committee on restructuring the state (CRS) proposed 14 provinces and 22 ethnic clusters as autonomous regions Nepali politics remained divided between pro-ethnic and anti-ethnic federalism even without trying to understand what ethnic federalism is for and what it is not. When the extended deadline of CA came closer the division of opinion on pro-ethnic and anti-ethnic lines became so pervasive that the key political actors almost lost the direction and CA was allowed to collapse.

Against this background this paper seeks to make an appraisal of the state of federalism discourse in Nepal. The paper begins with briefly highlighting the federal principles and practices in the global context so that it can set the conceptual outlines in which I have based my understanding of federalism and its different aspects relating to Nepal. Second, the paper explores how the idea of federalism had been floated and began to take shape in Nepal's political discourse and its contributing elements. It also takes into account of various ideas and proposals put forth by individual authors, political parties and the groups advocating federalism. Finally, the paper analyses the impact that the discourses have had on the constitution making process in CA and particularly major political parties' responses to it.

Federalism: Principles and Practices

Federalism is defined as a system of polity in which at least two levels of government - national and regional - are maintained over the same land and people. And spheres of governmental activities and powers are divided among such units by a constitutional arrangement. No encroachment of each other's sphere is allowed. The constituent units enjoy autonomy enough to regulate their affairs and maintain distinct identity within the federation. The federation as a whole or as represented by the federal union for that matter is treated as a sovereign political entity and enjoys the status of undivided sovereign country in the international arena. Historically federalism has come into existence and evolved in different contexts peculiar to the country concerned. But in recent decades it has been linked with the political management of diversities in a given political

a constitution based on federalism. This implied that CA had an overwhelming mandate for making a federal constitution for Nepal.

society so as to minimize the conflicts emanating from diversities relating to ethnicity, language, culture, geographic regions and so on.

In conventional political science literature and constitutional studies, federation means an association of relatively autonomous states (constituent units) in the given national state in which the governmental institutions and functions are territorially divided into two levels, both acting independently in their respective spheres (Anderson, 2008; Riker, 1975; Watts, 2008). It blends the idea of 'self-rule' at the constituent units' level and the 'shared-rule' at the federal level through written constitutional arrangements. The constitution guarantees that there will be no encroachment of each others' sphere. In order to change it constitutional amendment is required in which the constituent units have also a role. However, 'the existence of a single, indivisible yet composite federal nation' is simultaneously admitted (Duchacek, 1970:192).

Federalism has been in general adopted in the societies that are normally large in size and multinational in character. So, most of the larger countries of the world, except China, have adopted the federal system. But it does not necessary mean that federalism is less relevant to smaller countries. There are many countries (8 out of 26) smaller than Nepal having federal system. The smaller countries in most cases have adopted federalism as a response to internal diversity and as an instrument to manage the conflicts emanating from differences due to ethnicity, language, geographic region, etc.

Modern federal states with certain level of continuity began in 1789 when the US constitution was adopted though it has used the term 'Union' instead of federation. Switzerland entered into federal arrangement in 1848 but continues to use the term 'confederation' (Linder, 2010). Older federations such as in the United States and Switzerland emerged as their respective constituent units voluntarily agreed to a sort of mutual compact through adoption of the federal constitution and entered into a new sovereign political entity without totally submitting their previous identity and autonomy as the self governing entities. The idea behind such 'coming together' and forming the federation was motivated by the urge for creating a larger political entity in order to assure greater prosperity because they realized that the strength lies in unity rather than the independent sovereign but divided units. Canada and Australia formed federations as a deal between the British government and the colonial settlers, since both of them were under the British authority. The independence of both Canada and Australia also coincided with the adoption of federal constitution.

Many countries in the American continent such as Argentina, Brazil, Mexico, Venezuela, also adopted federal system soon after the independence in the nineteenth century. However, their experiment with federalism did not have sustained evolution as democracy was frequently upset in these countries. Again in the 1980s and 1990s they revived federalism along with the restoration of democracy. With the resurgence of independence and democracy in the 1950s and 1960s many Asian and African countries such as India, Pakistan, Malaysia, Nigeria, also chose the federal system while designing their respective constitutions. The existence of semi-independent states and the pattern of colonial administration provided them some basis for federal structure in addition to the ethno-regional diversities of the population. In the later decades Spain, Belgium, Ethiopia and South Africa also transformed to the federal structure in order to manage their internal diversity related conflicts.

In the late twentieth century, the countries in different regions of the world witnessed growing violent ethnic conflicts and divisive trends and it was in that context federalism gained a renewed importance to deal with cultural diversities, competitive ethno-territorial identities and claims in multi-cultural and multi-ethnic states. Federalism has thus become political tools in the post-conflict constitutional engineering in many countries. In most cases it has been used as "institutional, legal and democratic instruments to prevent violent minority conflicts" (Gunther, 1997). The countries like Spain, Belgium, Ethiopia, fall into this category. Besides, federalism has been an attractive appeal since it provides for small governments with ample scope 'for accommodation of all views, political compromise and the value of community' (Inman and Rubinfeld, 1997). In most cases in recent time, the federalization occurred as a process of disaggregating the unitary structure into several self-governing territorial units as they wanted "to express distinctive identities through smaller, directly accountable self-governing political units able to give expression to historical, social, linguistic or cultural identity" (Watts and Kincaid, 2008). Nepal's decision to go for federalism is also a part of such exigency.

The federalism debate in the world has a long history. It could be traced back even long before the modern federations such as those of US, Switzerland, Canada or Australia came into existence (Friedrich, 1968).

Federalism both as idea and political system have been debated among the practitioners and academics of various disciplines, e.g., political scientists, constitutional lawyers, political anthropologists, development experts, etc. A wide body of literature has already been produced and continues to proliferate in different aspects of federal theories and practices, and sharing of ideas and experiences on the working of federal systems in various countries. So internationally federalism discourse is a continuous process accommodating the emerging ethno-regional political trends and dynamics.

Soon after the end of World War II and the resurgence of independence movement in Asia and Africa and when ethnicity was yet to come in political prominence, William Livingston argued that diversities as the basis of federalism could cause an element of difference and might demand for 'self-expression'. He writes, "These diversities may be distributed among the members of a society in such a fashion that certain attitudes are found in particular territorial areas, or they may be scattered widely throughout the whole of the society. If they are grouped territorially, that is geographically, then the result may be a society that is federal." He has further noted that federalism "becomes nothing if it is held to embrace diversities that are not territorially grouped, for there are then no territorial units that can serve as components of the federal system" (Livingston, 1952: 86). Likewise, Duchacek (1970), Linder (2010), Gunther (1997), also treated federalism as the product of political management and distribution of governmental authorities to the territorial interest groups/ communities or sub-national units which would like to maintain their respective identities and autonomy as a national state. Thus the diverse territoriality of the constituent units makes the core of federal arrangement in a given political society.

As mentioned already towards the closing of twentieth century federalism received a renewed relevance in the management of diverse societies whether it is geographically a larger political unit or smaller one where the countries faced crises of division and disintegration. Ronald Watts states that federalism is "a practical way of combining the benefits of unity and diversity through representative institutions." Its application demands "a pragmatic, prudent approach" and institutional innovations. He emphasizes that in the emerging global context federalism as an idea could "provide a means for reconciliation" though it may not be a panacea

(Watts, 1998: 133).

Federalism discourse at the international level picked up a new height and dimension following the 1995 referendum result in which the issue of Quebec separation from Canada was rejected by a very narrow fraction of votes (the pro-unity received 50.6 per cent and pro-separatist received 49.4 percent of valid votes respectively). Though in the beginning it caused a sort of nervousness for the most Canadian politicians and academics but ultimately proved a catalytic factor to generate a new series of innovative debate on federalism, which as Bob Rae called it as the "resurgence of the federal idea" which occurred towards the closing of twentieth century "owing to the vitality of the values of democracy, revolution of the politics of identity and human rights" (Rae, 2003). Then the debate kicked off and federalism received a global attention.

However, the federal debate in the global level has received a new momentum as in recent decades with various problems both in the advanced countries like Canada and Switzerland where federalism has been practiced since quite a long time as well as the Afro-Asian countries in political transition due to internal political crises or for other reasons. Particularly in such countries where contesting claims by various ethno-regional groups having multiethnic composition and the conflicts emanating from it. This also brought together the federal countries to learn from each other leading towards the formation of the Forum of Federations in 1998 at international level and since 1999 international conferences have become regular feature of global dialogue on federalism.[3] Such conferences are meant for "learning from each other in an intensive exchange of ideas, thoughts and experiences, and to develop possible solutions together." (Koller, 2003: 4). However, to quote Ronald Watts again, the challenge before the scholars as well as the practitioners of federalism is 'to contribute, by critical, objective, and comparative analysis, to a better understanding of how new federal system may be established or existing ones made more effective' (Watts, 1998: 133). Koller stresses that "a federal political culture" is required to make the federal experiment sustainable and successful. According to him such a culture calls for "mutual trust, a readiness for mutual dialogue between diverse but equal partners, loyalty towards the federal government, and a consensus that diversity is an enrichment of the

---

3   Since 1999 there have been five international conferences and the fifth one was held in Ethiopia in December 2010.

federal state rather than a threat to the state's integrity (Koller, 2003: 6).

Federalism Discourse in Nepal

The logic for federalism in Nepal has three major grounds: (i) the plural and diverse composition of Nepali society, (ii) strengthening democracy from the bottom, and (iii) speeding up development process in a more equitable and efficient manner. For the second and third reasons, federalism may not be an essential criterion and can be achieved even under unitary state. However, Nepal's experience for more than half a century did not yield such result. But the aspirations for identity and autonomy can be best assured under federalism. Nepali society is so diverse and plural that requires multi-layer polity in order to strengthen the sense of national belonging among the diverse communities. Federalisation of the polity is considered as an accepted solution to this problem. It is therefore a new process of reordering state-society relationship based on democratic principles and recognition of community rights.

Nepal's discourse on federalism is of recent origin, but it thrived so quickly in a short span of time which hardly allowed any informed debate and reasoning that would lead towards forging minimum consensus on the federal design. The discourse was heavily dominated by ethno-regional emotion that no major political parties could afford either to ignore or fully embrace it. Even the Unified Communist Party of Nepal (Maoist) (UCPNM)[4] which has extended its organizational platform as a pro-ethnic party could not come in a decisive way to the adoption of a federal constitution when CA was finally struggling to overcome on the federalism issues and let CA accomplish its principal job of constitution making.

For the analytical purpose of this paper Federalism discourse in Nepal could be divided into four phases – the genesis of the idea, the demand phase, the proposal phase, and the negotiating phase. However, in terms of timing these phases overlap so massively that it often becomes almost impossible to make a distinction that which phase and timing we are talking for.

---

4   After CA election the Communist Party of Nepal (Maoist) and Jana Morcha Nepal merged and the party was renamed as UCPNM. However in June 2012 after the end of CA tenure the faction led by Mohan Baidya formed a new party calling CPN-Maoist. For the purpose of this paper whenever the term 'Maoist' is used as a party it refers to CPNM or UCPNM as per the sequence and context.

The voice for federalism in Nepal was first raised in the early 1950s when the country had for the first time witnessed the introduction of democracy after the overthrow of the century-old family oligarchy. Some of the Tarai elite who felt excluded in the new power structure had formed a party called Tarai Congress on the regional basis claiming to represent the Tarai region, the southern part of Nepal bordering India, which is now popularly called as 'Madhes', and demanded for a separate province comprising that region as "an autonomous Tarai state" comprising the parts of southern Nepal below the *chure* hills (Devakota, 1959; Yadav, 2003).

Likewise, about the same time the Limbu reform activists in the eastern hills also demanded for "Limbuwan autonomous province" (Baral and Tilega Limbu, 2064 BS[5]). Limbus of eastern Nepal claim that Prithvi Narayan Shah, who founded the present state of Nepal in the latter half of the eighteenth century could not conquer their area and had to accede autonomy to them in exchange of allegiance to the newly founded Kingdom. However that autonomy was gradually destroyed in the later years by the Rana rulers and the Panchayat regime. The Limbuwan activists assert that this provides them the historical basis for federalism and justify the claim for 'autonomous Limbuwan' province. However, they too did not talk of federalism in an overall context of the country.

These early voices for federalism did not sustain and the overall politics of the country was engulfed by the nationalist ideological platform even in the 1950s when some elements of democracy were in practice. Later on it was almost impossible to make such expressions in the regime that followed after the Royal Takeover in 1960. Besides, some of the leaders who had raised the voice for federalism in the 1950s submitted to the royal regime and enjoyed power. It was only after the restoration of democracy in 1990 the aspirations for language rights, ethnic identity and regional autonomy began to reassert. Some of the political parties formed after 1990 such as Nepal Sadbhabana Party, Rashtriya Janamukti Party had raised the voice for federalism in Nepal. These parties and ethnic organizations had made submissions to the Constitution Reform Commission in favour of federal system in Nepal. These demands did not have significant impact on the constitution making and initiating the

---

5 Most publications in Nepali language in Nepal use Nepali era called as *Bikram Sambat* (BS). Use of BS in citation in this article therefore refers to Nepali era.

federalism discourse at that time. However, the 1990 constitution declared Nepal a 'multiethnic, multilingual' Kingdom accepting the ethnic and linguistic diversity of the country (1990 Constitution: Article 4).

Taking the advantage of democracy various ethnic organizations were formed including their umbrella organization – Nepalese Federation of Indigenous Nationalities (NEFIN), which ultimately proved a strong rallying platform for ethnic mobilization all over the country. In the beginning NEFIN demands were basically for language rights, secularism, recognition of ethnic identity, proportional representation, inclusion, etc, The state also tried to response these voices by allowing government controlled media to broadcast news in different languages, recognizing ethnic groups as indigenous people and listed fifty-nine such groups, established the National Foundation for Development of Indigenous Nationalities in 2002 to promote the welfare of these groups. Besides, a special policy and programme was launched for indigenous people with Ninth Plan (HMG/N, 2055 BS). However, these measures were considered too little and NEFIN continued to mobilize the ethnic solidarity for achieving its demands. However till 2001 federalism was not seen as the demand influencing the ethnic activists and academics.[6]

The federalism debate began to pick up its motion with visible impact after the CPNM formed various ethnic fronts in order to mobilize people's support to their armed insurrection in late 1990s. Accordingly, some of the communism inclined writers and ethnic activists began to float the idea of 'autonomous region' on ethnic line (Neupane, 2000; Yonjan 2004; Gurung, 2004; Shrestha, 2004; Thapa, 2005). In the course of insurgency the CPNM had declared 9 autonomous regions in the country and also announced the establishment of such regions as their parallel governance structure (K.C, 2060 BS). In the concept paper prepared for the dialogue with the government CPNM had proposed four-tier structure – centre, autonomous region, district and municipality/village levels (CPNM, 2003). These debates and initiatives rarely used the term federalism and visibly lacked its acceptance too because the activists were of the communist ideological background (Sherchan, 2004:74).

Obviously, the Maoist official documents had no mention of

6 This could be seen in the report of NEFIN activities on the occasion of World Indigenous Day August 9, 2001 in which except Mahendra Lawoti's paper none the commenter or the participant from the floor had raised the voice for federalism (NEFIN, 2003).

federalism *per se*, except 'autonomous region' which does not necessarily mean federalism. In those documents the influence of Lenin's notion of 'nationality', 'national self-determination' and the Chinese experiment with 'autonomous region' for the minority ethnic groups could be found. Such expressions had therefore more affiliation with Leninist ideas and communism than the federal democratic principles. However, all these notions and ideas proved quite effective to mobilize ethnic sentiments and energized the ethnic solidarity which ultimately led to the demand that ethnicity should be the core of federal design for Nepal when CA sat for writing the constitution.

The terminologies that the Maoist used borrowing from Lenin such as 'oppressed nationalities', 'oppressor nationality', 'right to self-determination', and some coined in Nepali context as 'Khas/Hindu hegemony', etc. became quite popular among the ethnic scholars as well as activists. Similarly the Maoist opposition to Sanskrit education had also appealed to the ethnic activists as a strategy to attack Hindu caste elitism and the domination of Nepali language. Leading ethnic scholar cum activists found that the Maoist's stand on ethnic issues as close and identical to those of *Janajatis*. Their writings also massively used these terminologies particularly to describe the interface between the Nepali state and ethnic groups (Subba, 2006; Bhattachan, 2000; Lawoti, 2005; Mabuhang, 2059 BS; Sherchan, 2004; Tamang, 2066 BS).

These aspirations and demands owing to the diversity of Nepali society that began to surface from the beginning of this millennium has been termed by the Nepali writers and analysts as "restructuring of the state" (Sharma, 2060 BS; Khanal, 2061 BS: Baral, 2061 BS). This was formally included in the agenda of mainstream parliamentary political parties when they formed 'Seven Party Alliance' (SPA) in 2005 to resist the royal authoritarianism as the former king Gyanendra had further sidelined them and imposed his direct rule. And this phrase was also included in 12-point understanding between CPNM and SPA reached at New Delhi in November 2005. The understanding stated that the restructuring the state had been inevitable in order to resolve the problems relating to class, ethnicity, gender and regions. It was reiterated further in the Comprehensive Peace Accord (CPA) reached between the Government of Nepal (GoN) and CPNM a year later in November 2006 following the success of *Jana Andolan II* in April 2006 (Clause 3.5/CPA, 2006).

The Interim Constitution (IC) which was promulgated in January 2007 finally made a constitutional commitment to restructure the state in order to end the discrimination based on ethnicity, language, religion, culture, region, gender, etc. For this purpose it also provided that a State Restructuring Commission would be formed to make suggestions in this matter and the final settlement would be made by CA. Federalism was not yet explicitly mentioned as the basis of restructuring the state. This provoked a strong reaction from the Madhesi community and the ethnic groups. Soon after the promulgation of IC a revolt in Madhes sparked off which ultimately pressurized the state to accept that federalism would be the basis of state restructuring and accordingly the interim constitution was amended which stated that the restructuring of the state will be done in line with "democratic federal system". This followed a series of ethno-regional movements by Madhesi, Janajati activists and the government had accordingly accepted their demands relating to federalization of the state. The Fifth Amendment to Interim Constitution in July 2008 stated the restructuring of the state in following words:

Accepting the aspirations of indigenous ethnic groups and the people of the backward and other regions, and the people of Madhes, for autonomous provinces, Nepal shall be a Federal Democratic Republic. The provinces shall be autonomous with full rights. The Constituent Assembly shall determine the number, boundary, names and structures of the autonomous provinces and the distribution of powers and resources, while maintaining the sovereignty, unity and integrity of Nepal. (Article 138(1a)/IC).

Thus Nepal formally decided to transform the existing unitary state into a federal one. This followed the proliferation of writings on federalism in Nepal which mostly dealt on the various aspects of especially its principles and the basis of creating provinces (Baral, 2064 BS; Baral, 2009; Hachhethu, 2009; Khanal, 2008; 2065BS, 2064 BS; Mabuhang, 2064 BS; Sharma, 2064 BS). Elections for the Constituent Assembly (CA) were held in April 2008 in which most of the political parties campaigned for the federal republican system and won most seats in an assembly of 601 members. Rashtriya Jana Morcha (National People's Front), which campaigned against federalism, won only 4 seats. Thus the CA had an overwhelming mandate to frame the new constitution on the basis of federal republican line. And the government was expected to chalk out the course of transition from unitary to federal state.

Accordingly CA started its work on constitution making soon it adopted the Rules and formed thematic committees to make preliminary drafts. The Committee on Restructuring the State and Distribution of State Power Committee (CRS) was assigned to prepare the preliminary draft of the new constitution relating to federalism such as demarcating the geographic areas, naming and number of the provinces, distribution of powers between the centre and provinces and other layers of government, mechanisms to resolve the disputes, etc. CRS began its work with the calling for suggestions from the citizens, political parties, civil society and any other organizations and individuals interested to make their submissions to this effect. This coincided with mushrooming of ideas and proposals relating to the federal design. Several models were floated by the political parties, ethnic communities, civil society organizations, individual citizens, etc. Ethnic activists had demanded for the formation of the provinces on ethnic line, a sort of 'ethnic homeland' based on their historic territories with a provision of '*agradhikar*' (the preferential right for the ethnic community to head the government in their respective provinces). Contrary to this the non-ethnic groups argued that the provinces should be carved out taking into account of the mixed pattern of the settlement of population and Nepal's economic and development reality. Likewise, the madhes-centric parties and groups had demanded a separate province of 'one madhes' comprising the entire Tarai region from east to west. As a counter to this some groups demanded for a separate province comprising the entire *chure bhabar* region from east to west, parallel to Madhes. Similarly in the northern mountain region some groups demanded for 'Himali autonomous region' from east to west.

Nepal's process of federalization as elsewhere involves three major but interrelated dimensions - identification of territorial units that would form provinces of the new federation; multi-level division of power and distribution of jurisdictional authority; and maintenance of unity and stability as a national state consistent with federal values and culture. The crafting of provinces also required to respect for the aspiration for ethno-regional identity of the concerned population groups. This would demand immense homework with sound technical backup. It was the foremost challenge. But unfortunately there was no serious move to this direction.

Although some historical ethno-regional pockets do exist in Nepal they have had been diluted by the pattern of internal migration and the unitary political and administrative structure of the state over centuries. A tendency of pre-Gorkha conquest revivalism heavily marked the territorial claims of the proposed provinces by ethnic activists and organizations which caused a fear of fragmentation of the country into ethnic clusters and weakening the very existence of the national state. Opinion also extremely differed in number and name of the proposed federal units, and so the division of powers between the centre and the units particularly in the matters relating to natural resources and revenue sharing.

Hundreds of proposals were floated by various political parties, ethnic organizations/ activists, experts, and so. Most of the parties represented in CA (15 out of 25) submitted their respective federal designs including the names and geographic areas of the proposed provinces. CPNM had campaigned for CA elections with a map of federal Nepal with 11 provinces and three sub-provinces (CPNM, 2064 BS) while most other parties had just outlined the principles federal design and bases for creating the provinces. Madhes-based parties had campaigned for one madhes province comprising the entire tarai region in the south. When CA started its business most political parties having representation in CA submitted their design of federal Nepal with proposed provinces. CPN-UML had proposed 15 provinces in the beginning and NC did not officially put forth any such design but its members at CRS submitted dissenting note with the provincial designs (CRS, 2066). However, most of them were relating to the names, numbers and territory of the provinces and less on other important aspects of federalism such as the mechanism for power sharing, i.e., the 'shared rule', the distribution of competencies or power among different layers of government, especially between the federation and provinces, representation in the upper house, coordination and dispute settlement mechanisms, etc.

A cursory look at these proposals would show that the proposed number of provinces ranged from 3 to 15. All these proposals may broadly be classified into five categories: (i) views relating to political parties and their respective lines, (ii) views reflecting ethnic organizations and movement, (iii) those relating to madhes-centric, (iv) those relating to non-ethnic and development centric, and (v) those relating to geographic regions and devolution of powers (Khanal, 2066 BS). However, the opinion was finally divided between the so-called "pro-ethnic" or single identity-based 'ethnic federation' and "non-ethnic" or multiple identity based federation.

Those floating ethnicity-based provinces or autonomous regions had focused to cover major ethno-regional clusters and came up with proposals between 8 to 14 provinces in number. UCPNM had taken a lead to propagate it and other minor parties, inclined to communist ideology and ethnicity as their organizing principles also followed the suit. They included CPN (integrated), Rashtriya Janamukti Party, Shanghiya Loktantrik Rashtriya Munch, Samajwadi Prajatantrik Party, etc. However the pro-ethnic camp was spearheaded by NEFIN and other related ethnic networks than political parties. Madhes-centric parties like Madhesi Jana Adhikar Forum, Tarai-Madhes Lokatantrik Party and Sadbhabana Party proposed three-province model based on mountain, hill and tarai regions with necessary sub-provinces in the respective regions. Moreover, they were least concerned about the nature and number of provinces in the hills.

Other parties were divided in between the idea taken by UCPNM and NC. NC was for fewer (six or seven) provinces based on some geographic features and demography. CPN (UML) remained divided but the dominant leadership joined with NC's approach. Some smaller left inclined parties like CPN (ML), Nepal Majdur Kisan Party, though supported federalism in principle during CA elections appeared to a regional devolution of power approach rather than federalism as such. RPP, RPP Nepal, CPN (united) though in CA election manifestos had expressed support to federalism in principle but declined to support the idea in CA business and demanded that the issue should be referred to national referendum.

It was against this background CA committee on state restructuring (CRS) proposed a 14-province model with majority vote. This model proposed a three-tier structure – federal, provincial and local government with the list of their respective competencies. Though the committee had unanimously approved 'identity and viability' to be the principal criteria for creating the provinces the members and the parties on the number, name and boundary of the provinces. The CSR proposed 14-province model was heavily criticized as propagating ethnic federalism in Nepal and was rejected by NC and other parties. The committee had proposed special preferential right to some of the ethnic groups in heading the government in their respective provinces and autonomous regions which contained the elements of ethnic federalism. With this the federalism discourse in

Nepal entered into new dimension marked by pro-ethnic vs anti-ethnic sentiments.

The State Restructuring Commission as provided by the interim constitution was formed very late, (i.e. third week of November 2011) as if it was only to meet the technicality of the constitutional provision rather than seeking genuine recommendations. This was also reflected in the selection of its members who from the very beginning remained divided on party line and could not make a consensus report. Consequently the Commission's recommendations also became highly controversial. A separate report was submitted by the minority group. The majority report resembled the position taken by UCPN and Madhesi parties whereas the minority report those of NC and UML. The Commission's majority report contrary to CA Committee had reduced the number of provinces to 10 and also dropped the preferential right of ethnic group to head the government in the provinces (HLSRC, 2068 BS), which were considered as 'positive', but in the boundaries, names and proposal for non-territorial province for Dalits were very much disputed. This sparked a prolonged strike in the far west region and nation-wide protest by Khas Chhetri, Brahman and Dasnami groups as well as Madhesi and Janjatis' counter protests in favour of identity based provinces became a regular features when the leaders started exploring the agreed solution to the federal design.

Already following the country's declaration to go for federalism in January 2007 in general and SRC's 14-province model in particular had sparked reactions of both in favour and against particularly through the media. Besides, some leading experts on Nepali affairs both national and international had also expressed their views in different aspects of federalism both in favour and against. In this paper I have tried to pick up some representative opinion and ideas particularly from the perspective of pro-ethnic and non-ethnic or anti-ethnic federalism discourses.

If we look at the views expressed for pro-ethnic or identity based federalism they seem supportive to 14-province model as proposed by CRS or the 12-province model as proposed by Indigenous Peoples (IP) Caucus (2068 BS) at CA (Lawoti 2011; Manadhar, 2011; Mabuhang, 2011). They argued that the debate for or against 'ethnic federalism' in Nepal is redundant. Recognition of identity as the basis of federalism in Nepal is relevant and is necessary to end the centuries of Hill/Hindu Chhetri-Brhamin hegemony. In the same vein, Yash Ghai who had the role of advising UNDP on Nepal's constituent assembly affairs before CA elections (2006-2008), also opines that IPs' thrust for federalism in Nepal is to end the hegemony of particular communities, particularly Bahun/ Chhetri in political mainstream (Ghai, 2011). Krishna Hachhethu, who had served as State Restructuring Commission member, also admits that the main purpose of state restructuring in Nepal is to end the centuries of Hindu high caste domination but refutes that federalism as proposed by the commission and CA committee as being 'ethnic federalism'. In his opinion these are 'ethnic in appearance, but not in essence' (Hachhethu, 2012). Prof. Lok Raj Baral also holds the view that there is no harm to accept 'more small provinces' for better participation of the people (Baral, 2012).

Contrarily, there are opinion that the proposals made by CA committee and the commission were of ethnicity based federalism and for them it does not suit Nepal's reality and in some cases it is illogical too because "there is no fixity of permanence to it" (Mishra, 2011). For ending the discrimination there could be several other affirmative options, not necessarily the 'ethnic federalism'. Some even fear that it would open the door for 'centrifugal tendencies' undermining the national state (Lohani, 2011). Those who contradict with ethnicity based provincial design proposes north-south model or diluting the ethno-regional boundaries (Adhikari,2066 BS; Thapa, 2066BS; Chongwang, 2063 BS). But it is also argued that the north-south model of province does not help "to move ahead by neglecting present day political realities" (Sharma, 2011). Some opine that provinces should be based on river basin and in that case Nepal does not need more than three provinces (Bohara, 2065 BS; Shrestha, 2011). Some foreign scholars who have been watching Nepal since quite a long time also see ethnic federalism as less relevant for Nepal (Gellner, 2011).

If we go by the opinion as expressed through the media the dominant tendency is ethnic polarization of the opinion and ideas. It is not necessary that all janajati writers opine for pro-ethnic provinces nor all hill Brahman Chhetri subscribe to anti-ethnic approach. The same applies to Madhesis about one or several provinces in Tarai/Madhes. As Prashant Jha writes that the demand for federalism "has emerged and been articulated as group rights. Economic viability is important, and it is unwise to have a state in places which do not have single township, big hospital, or a single university or the minimum population to sustain it." He also opines that preferential right violates democratic principles.(Jha, 2011).

Against the above background the leaders of major political parties finally sat for resolving the federalism related disputes in the beginning of May 2012. Neither the CA committee's 14-province nor the commission's 10-province model was acceptable to all the parties. Therefore they tried to develop new options agreeable to all, at least to the so called major political parties – UCPNM, NC, UML and Madhesi Democratic Front. The number and names were the major disputes. NC had proposed 7 provinces keeping all 75 district boundaries intact, UML 12, and UCPNM 10 provinces model. But each rejected the others. It was reported that in the middle of May they had reached to an agreement on 11-provinces (four in Madhes and 7 in hills) model that all provinces would be multiethnic and citizens of any ethnicity, caste, religion, region, language, culture, etc. would have equal rights in any province relating to economic, social, cultural fields. The names were to be decided by the elected respective provincial assemblies. And a federal commission was also proposed to determine the details.' (*Nagarik*, 16 May 2012). The Madhesi democratic front despite reservation had also given positive signals to it by saying not to disrupt the constitution making process only on that ground but soon both Madhesi and janajati activists began to protest it. A large groups of CA members (320) both from janajati and madhesi belonging to different political parties including those of NC and UML threatened to reject that deal generating lot of pressure to their respective parties and leaders (*Kantipur* 20 May 2012). Puspa Kamal Dahal 'Prachanda' provoked the janajati activists to go to the street for identity based provinces (*Nagarik*, 21 May 2012).

On the eve of CA close down the government had reached into agreements with various agitating groups contradicting its positions one after another. On 17th May it had made a deal with Brahmin Chhetri groups and those from far west to respect for undivided region and recognized them as IP. On 22 May again the government made a deal with agitating IP groups agreeing on identity based provinces. (*Nagarik* 23 May 2012). Behind the scene when CA deadline was about to end there had been a lot of flexibility from all sides including IP and Madhesi accepting 'multiple identities' as the basis for creating the provinces. Even NC was prepared to accept 13-province model in that case. But at the end nothing prevailed except to end CA without agreeing for next alternative. NC and UML withdrew from the government and the remaining coalition partners mainly UCPNM and Madhesi front decided to hold the election for new CA in November 2012 pushing the country in political limbo.

Geo-politics and federalism

After the end of CA it became clearer that Nepal's choice for federalism has geopolitical limitations too. One can assume that highly ethnicized federalism discourse in Nepal had been quietly watched by both the neighbours without explicit reactions until CA was doing its business. Even when CA process continued it was reported India's Foreign Secretary Runjan Mathai and his South Bloc authorities including Akhilesh Mishra who looks Nepal affairs while talking to visiting Nepali journalists had told that federalization process is a "complex" issue and 'needs to accommodate the voices of groups relating to ethnicity and regionalism' (*Kantipur*, 22 May 2011). But it began to express in a more explicit form after the end of CA.

India herself has adopted the federal system and for many Nepalis tend to believe that federalism in Nepal should be its priority. Some irresponsible expressions from certain quarters often gives such impression as the Indian Consular based in Birgunj was reported to have expressed reservation on the division of Tarai into several provinces and had Madhesi politicians to protest when leaders were floated a tacit understanding on 11-province model. (*Kantipur*, 18 May 2012). However, the Indian authorities should be well known of the cross border ethno-regional and cultural affinities and its political implications. Nepal's situation is very much common to India's Northeast region where 40 million people belong to some 200 ethnic groups having cross border ethnic affinity with Bangladesh and Myanmar. Their "historical connections with India are nebulous and affinities with Southeast Asia are perhaps stronger." (Moolankkattu and Singh, 2011: 457-458).

Soon after the end of CA the former Indian Ambassador to Nepal, Shiva Shankar Mukharjee in an interview told to the Kantipur daily (12 June 2012) that it was quite natural for madhesi, janajati to assert power. But implying to the western countries' support for federal agenda he commented that these countries did not know the reality of Nepal. What they are doing in Nepal though might not appear as 'interference' it was intended to 'influence' Nepal's affairs. He also opined that Nepal should go for parliamentary elections rather than the CA. Likewise, Jayanta Prasad, the Indian Amabssador, also opined that creating the provinces on the basis of ethnicity should be problamatic therefore it should be based on economic and social consideration (*Kantipur*, 2 September 2012).

But the northern neighbor – People's Republic of China seemed more nervous with Nepal's federalism and the federal proposals. How this concern was expressed and communicated to Nepali leaders until CA was working was not very much known. But after the end of CA the Chinese concern has been expressed in unequivocal terms. The visiting Chinese delegation a month after the collapse of CA under the leadership of Ai Ping, the Vice Minister for Asian Affairs in the International Relations Department of Communist Party of China was reported to have expressed concern over Nepal going for federalism and suggested to achieve through decentralization. He was reported even to have warned the international agencies (the Western and Indian) not to provoke ethnicity in Nepal (*Annapurna Post*, 1 July 2012; *Rajdhani*, 1 July 2012; Ghimire, 2012). This concern was further elabourated in the writings of leading journalists. To quote, Sudhir Sharma, "China, through political, diplomatic, academic (Think Tank) channels had repeatedly given advice to the high level Nepali leaders including Prachanda that single identity based federalism is not in the interest of Nepal which ultimately would also be against the interest of China. What Ai Peng told in June after the end of CA was only the reiteration of it to the four top leaders in a way known to the public at large." (Sharma, 2012).

Conclusion

The collapse of CA after four years of exercise is a political failure. Whom to be blamed? Politics of blaming each other has already started which is but natural in politics. Several questions arise which need further research and analysis. When the time to transform the country into federal structure came nearer the leaders were expected to rise above the sloganeering phase of federalism and translate it into political reality. But they failed to moderate their stands. It is still a subject to thorough research why CA was dissolved. Whether it was due to the parties' inability to come to the understanding of federal design or they were compelled to abandon the federal idea on that excuse.

Apparently it is a fact that CA ended because the political leaders could not reach to an amicable model of federalism. It is not so simple to be convinced. A reluctant approach to federalism was there from the very beginning. The delay in the formation of State Restructuring Commission by the government, irrespective of who led the government, is self evident. But the whole politics of the country had swept by a federalist wave either for populist purpose or with some genuine reasons. But deeper in the mainstream politics due to too much ethnicization of the issues, had caused concerns and crisis of confidence even among those leaders who proclaimed to be the 'federalist'. Lack of self-convinced and daring leadership is the most visible reason for this tragic end to federal destiny.

Obviously, Nepal is not free of its geo-political location it is bound to be influenced by it in an explicit or implicit manner. On federalism also this factor seemed to have played a decisive role.. Perhaps, the top leaders were aware of this limitations which they could neither make public nor possess the skill to manage it. There were attempts and strategies to postpone the federal agenda indirectly as the leaders continued to float the idea of bringing the constitution without federalism because of time constrain and due to the complexity of the issues, that federal component could be added later. But due to the apprehensions of possible madhesi and janajti outburst severely constrained the leaders to choose that option. Therefore delaying the constitution making process seemed to be a deliberate strategy. In order to put off the federalism CA was bound to collapse and a period of four years was quite exhaustive for the people to feel relief.

Putting off federal agenda might ultimately invite more risk than the relief. A new dynamics of constitutional crisis has already crept in questioning the very legitimacy of whatever action that the government takes having political implications. The clash for power without mandate and legitimacy or very short-term exigency is going to be the game of politics. However, the ultimate looser would be the political parties.

Whether it is an election for next CA or the parliament federalism is sure to come up again. Already national political parties like NC and UML have been threatened to lose the support of the ethnic and madhesi community. Next may be the turn of UCPNM. Such a polarization would have serious implications not only for national political parties but also for the national solidarity. This would also be a heavy cost to democracy as well. Politics may turn to an authoritarian path which is already in the course.

The federal discourses continue despite the end of CA. This is also a time to have an introspection of it. While designing the federal structures particularly the provincial design the leaders as well those engaged in federalism discourses need to take into account the sensitivity of all particularly affecting the national harmony, geopolitical sensitivity, ethnic sentiments of all people. Federalism is for all the Nepalis irrespective of their ethno-regional origins and identity therefore, it should accordingly be able to recognize this fact. The discourses need to be informed, objective as well reason based. Of course, sentiment and emotions are very much part of it but equally important it to make it mutually respecting and tolerant.

References

Adhikari, Bipin (2065). *Nepalko Namuna Sambidhan*. Kathmandu: Sambidhan Bisheshagyan samuha.

Anderson, George (2008). *Federalism: An Introduction*. Ontario: Oxford University Press.

Baral, Bhavani (2061 BS). *Yesto hunuparchha rajyako samrachana*, Swattya shasan sarokar mancha.

Baral, Bhabani and Kamal Tilega Limbu (2008). *Limbuwanko Rajniti (Itihas. Bartman ra Dastabej*. Dharan: Bikalpa Prakashan.

Baral, Lok Raj (2012). "Face the Facts", *The Kathmandu Post*, 21 May.

Baral, Lok Raj (2009). "Compulsions and Pitfalls" in *Nepali Journal of Contemporary Studies*, Vol. IX, No. 2, September.

Baral, (2064 BS). *Sanghiya Pranaliko Awashykata*. Lalitpur: Nepal Centre for Contemporary Studies (NCCS).

Bhattachan, Krishna B. (2000). "Possible Ethnic Revolution or Insurgency ina Predatary Unitary Hindu State, Nepal" in Dhruba Kumar edited *Domestic Conflict and Crisis of Governability in Nepal*. Kathmandu:

Centre for Nepal and Asian Studies (CNAS).

Bohara, Alok ((2065 BS). "Sanghiyatako bahas – Antarnirbhar model" *Himal*, 16-30 Srawan.

CA IP Caucus (2068 BS). *Sambidhansabhama bikshayagat samitiharuko prarambhik maseuda prativedanma Adibasi Janajati Sabhasadsabha (Caucus)ko samsodhan, parimarjan tatha tippanisahitko abhadharana, 2067*. Kathmandu: SPCBN/UNDP.

Chonghang, Harkaraj (2063). "Bahujatiya margachitra", Kantipur, 16 Asar.

Comprehensive Peace Accord 2063. Kathmandu: Ministry of Peace and Reconstruction, Government of Nepal, 2064 BS.

The Constitution of the Kingdom of Nepal 2047 (1990). Kathmandu: Ministry of Law, Justice and Parliamentary Affairs, His Majesty's Government/Nepal, 2001.

HMG/N (2055 BS). *Adibasi tatha Janajati Sambandhi Niti tatha Karyakrama*. Kathmaandu: National Planning Commiaaion,

CPNM (2003). *Proposal put forward by the CPNM for Negotiations*, April 27.

CSR (2066 BS), *Preliminary Draft Report including the concept notes*. Kathmandu: Restructuring the State and Distribution of State Power Committee, Constituent Assembly, Singha Durbar.

Devakota, Grisma Bahadur (1979). *Nepalko Rajnitik Darpan Part II*. Kathmandu: Dhruba Bahadur Devakota.

Duchacek, Ivo D. (1970). *Comparative Federalism The Territorial Dimension of Politics*. New York: Holt, Rinehart and Winston Inc.

Friedrich, Carl J. (1968). *Constitutional Government and Democracy*. New Delhi: Oxford & IBH Publishing Company (Indian Reprint, 1974).

Ghai, Yash (2011). "Ethnic Identity, Participation and Social Justice: A Constitution for New Nepal?". Martinus NJHOFF Publishers: *International Journal on Minority and Group Rights* 18 (2011), 309-334.

Gellner, David (2011). "Ethnic federalism saw disastrous consequences" in the interview to *Republica*. 30 April.

Ghimire, Yubraj (2012). "China's seniour leaders skips meeting Prime Minister", The *Reporter Weekly*, 1 July 2012.

Gunther, Bachler (1997) edited. *Federalism against Ethnicity?*. Zurich: Verlag Ruegger.

Gurung, K.B. (2004). "Rajyako Punarsamrachanako Awasyakata ra Nepalko Bishistatama Jatiya Kshetriya Swayattata" a paper presented at a seminar organized by akhil Nepal Janajati Sammelan, Kathmandu.

Hachhethu, Krishna (2012). "Clear Choice Federalism and Ethnicity", *Republica*, 21 March.

Hachhethu, Krishna (2009). *State Building in Nepal: Creating a Functional State*. Kathmandu: Enabling the State Programme (ESP).

HLSRC (2068 BS). *Recommendation Report of High-Level State Restructuring Recommendation Commission 2068*. Kathmandu.

Inman, Robert P. and Rubinfeld, Daniel L. (1997), "The political economy of federalism" in Dennis C Muller edited. *Perspectives on public choice*, Cambridge University Press, pp.73-105.

The Interim Constitution of Nepal 2063 (2007). Kathmandu: Ministry of Law Justice and Parliamentary Affairs, Government of Nepal, 2008.

Jha, Prashant (2011). "The Centrality of Identity", *The Kathmandu Post*, 7 December.

K.C., Sharad (2060 BS). "Maobadbata Jatibadatarpha", *Himal* Fortnightly16-30 Fagun, pp. 28-31.

Khanal, Krishna (2061 BS). *Rajyako Punarsamrachana : Ek Prastab*. Lalitpur: Nepal Centre for Contemporary Studies

Khanal, Krishna (2064 BS). "Shanghiya Rajya Samrachana: Manyata ra Abhyas" in *Nepalma Sanghiya Shasan Pranali Chunauti ra Awasarharu*. Kathmandu: National Peace Campaign.

Khanal, Krishna (2065 BS) edited. *Nepalma Sanghiya Shasan Pranali:*

Byabasthapan ra Karyanwayan, Kathmandu: National Peace Campaign.

Khanal, Krishna (2066 BS). *Sanghiya Ganarajya Nepalka lagi prastabit namunaharu : Ek tulanatmak bishleshana*. Kathmandu: National Peace Campaign. (An unpublished paper).

Khanal, Krishna P. "Restructuring of Nepali State The Federal Perspective" in Lok Raj Baral edited *Nepal – New Frontiers of Restructuring of State*. New Delhi: Adroit Publishers.

Koller, Arnold (2003), "Welcome Note" in Raoul Blindenbacher and Arnold Koller edited. *Federalism in a Changing World – Learning from Each Other*. Montreal & Kingston: McGill Queen's University Press, 2003.

Lawoti, Mahendra (2005). *Towards a Democratic Nepal Inclusive Political Institutions for a multicultural society*. New Delhi: Sage Publications.

Lawoti, Mahendra (2011). "Weighing the Options". *The Kathmandu Post*, 22 April

Linder, Wolf (2010). *Swiss Democracy* (Third Edition, revised and updated). London: Palgrave macmillan.

Livingston, William S. (1952). "A Note on the Nature of Federalism". *Political Science Quarterly*, Vol.67, No.1, March 1952, pp. 81-95.

Lohani, Prakash Chandra (2011). "On Ethnicity and Federalism". *Republica*, 28 March.

Mabuhang, Balkrishna (2011). "Bahundekhi Rautesamma Sanghiyata sambhava chha", *Kantipur*, 20 April.

Mabuhang, Balkrishna (2059 BS). "Bartaman Sandarbhama Nepalka Janajatiharu ke Chahanchhan?". *Mulyankana* 101. Pp. 22-24.

Mabuhang, Balkrishna (2064 BS). "Rajya Punarsamrachanaka lagi Sanghiya Shasan Pranali: Jatiya Janasankhiki Drishtikona" in *Nepalma Sanghiya Shasan Pranali Chunauti ra Awasarharu*. Kathmandu: National Peace Campaign.

Manadhar, Mangalsiddhi (2011). "Pahichan Nai mukhya Adhar", *Kantipur*, 28 April.

Mishra, Chaitanya (2011). "Ethnic Upsurge in Nepal: Implications for Federalization", A Draft paper presented at Symposium on Ethnicity and Federalism in Kathmandu, 22-24 April.

Moolakkattu, John S. and S. Mangi Singh (2011). "Identity Formation and Peace Building in Northeast India: An Introduction" in *Gandhi Marga.* Quarterly Journal of Gandhi Peace Foundation, New Delhi: Vol.32, No, 4, January-March, pp. 457-473.

NEFIN (2003). *Biswo Adibasi Diwas August 9, 2001 Prativedan.* Kathmandu: Nepal Janajati Mahasangh

Neupane, Govinda, *Nepalko Jatiya Prashna Samajik Banaut and Sajhedariko Sambhawna.* Kathmandu: Centre for Development Studies, 2000.

Rae, Bob (2005). "Foreword: The Resurgence of the Federal Idea" in Ann L. Griffiths edited (2005). *Handbook of Federal Countries, 2005.* Montreal & Kingston: McGill Queen's University Press.

Riker, William H (1975). "Federalism" in Fred I. Greenstein and Nelson W. Polsby (edited) *Handbook of Political Science,* Volume 5, Addison-Wesley Publishing Company.

Sharma, Pitamber (2011), "State restructuring report prepared without principles" in the interview to *Republica,* 4 July.

Sharma, Pitamber (2060). "Pradeshikata ra jatiya Sangh Auchitya ra Upadeyata", *Himal* 1-15 Chaita. pp. 18-20.

Sharma, Pitamber (2060). "Sanghiya Pranalika Adhar: Bhugol ra Yojanaparak Dristi" in *Nepalma Sanghiya Shasan Pranali Chunauti ra Awasarharu.* Kathmandu: National Peace Campaign.

Sharma, Pitamber and Narendra Khanal with Subhas Chaudhary Tharu (2009). *Towards A Federal Nepal An Assessment of Proposed Models.* Kathmandu: Himal Books.

Sharma, Sudhir (2012), "Beijingko Badalindo Najar", *Kantipur,* 4 July, 2012.

Sherchan, Sanjaya (2004). *Nepali Rajya ra Adibasi Janajati.* Kathmandu: Pasriha Garayoba.

Shrestha, Rajendra (2004). "Bahujatiya bahubhashik deshako rajya samrachanako sambandhama" (an unpublished paper).

Shrestha, Ratna Sansar (2011). "Jatiya adharma pranta banauda", *Gorakhapatra*, 18 April.

Subba, Chaitanya (2006). "The Ethnic Dimension of Maoist Conflict: Dreams and Design of Liberation of Oppressed Nationalities" in Lok Raj Baral edited. *Nepal Facets of Maoist Insurgency*. New Delhi: Adroit Publishers.

Tamang, Parasuram (2066). *Naya Sambidhan ra Alpasankhyak adibasi Janajti*. Kathmandu: Bibidh Pustak Bhandar.

Thapa, Pari (2005). "Bartaman Rajyako Punarsamrachana" a paper presented at NCCS workshop, Janaary and reproduced with updates in Sitaram Tamang edited. *Nepalko Sandarbhama Rajyako Punarsamrachana*. Kathmandu: Samana Prakashan Nepal, 2062 BS.

Thapa, Surya (2066 BS), "Sat Pradeshko Sundar Nepal", *Himal*, 1-15 Asar.

Watts, Ronald L. (2008). *Comparing Federal Systems*, Montreal: McGill-Queens University Press, 2008.

Watts, Ronald L. (1998). "Federalism, Federal Political System, and Federations". *Annual Reviews Political Science*. www. AnnualReview.org.

Watts, Ronald L and John Kinciad (2008). "Introduction" in John Kinciad and Rupak Chattopadhyay edited. *Unity in Diversity Learning from Each Other*, Volume 3. *Interaction in Federal Systems*. New Delhi: Viva Books.

Yadav, Upendra (2003). *Nepali Jana Andolan aur Madhesi Mukti ka Sawal*. Madhesi Peopls Right Forum, Nepal.

Yonjan Tamang, Kumar (2004). "Nepalko Bishistatama Swashasan: Kin ra Kasari?" Kathmandu: *Grengyam* (a monthly magazine related to indigenous nationalities) April.

Ethnic Conflict and Federalism in Nepal

Krishna Hachhethu

To bring an end to discrimination based on class, caste/ethnic, language, gender, culture, religion and region by eliminating the centralized and unitary form of the state, the state shall be made inclusive and restructured into a progressive, democratic federal system (The Interim Constitution of Nepal 2007).

Federalism has a potentiality to produce ethnic harmony as well as ethnic conflict. It could be an effective tool for management of social diversity. It could also fuel to intensify ethnic conflicts. Particularly in the formative phase of federal design in multi-ethnic state, it generally invites ethnic conflict. Nepal is the glaring example of transforming social diversity into political division over the issue of federal design. On the eve of the elections of the Constituent Assembly (CA) in May 2008, Madhesh based parties were formed with federal agenda that has resulted in reducing the influence of national political parties substantially in a region known as Tari or Madhesh. Madhesh spreads into nearly one forth of Nepal's territory where half of the total populations of the country live. Madheshis – including the people of plains Janajati, plains Dalit and Musalman – constitute 31 per cent of national population. After the termination of the CA in May 2012, formation of the Janajati based party is under process. Janajatis – a common title of officially recognized 59 indigenous nationalities – constitute 37 per cent of national population and most of them live in hill and mountain regions. The strength of Janajati based party can not be estimated at the moment but it obviously cuts the size of national political parties so far their support bases are concerned. The logic behind formation of Janajati based party is that national political parties are blamed for becoming hostile to their aspiration for setting ethnic identity based federalism. The hill castes people or Khas-Arya, including hill dalits – which constitutes 38 per cent of national population – are in forefront in opposing ethnic identity based federalism which was wrongly but deliberately propagated as ethnic federalism. They are vanguard for not allowing to mold the agenda of state restructuring beyond the shape of administrative or territorial federalism. Three major largest social groups of the country – Janajati, Madheshi and Khas-Arya – are in split on the model of Nepali federalism, the first two groups stand together for maximizing the ethnic and regional contents whereas the later opts for de-ethnicize the federal structure under making. The national political parties failed to reconcile between claims and counter claims of contested social groups vis-à-vis federalism. Eventually, caste/ethnic based polarization on federal question was transferred into political division in the CA. New political forces emerged since the election of the CA, i.e. the Maoist, Madheshi and Indigenous Peoples Caucus formally took a common position for ethnic identity based federalism but the traditional political parties, i.e. Nepali Congress (NC) and Communist Party of Nepal, Unified Marxist-Leninist (UML) in particular, opposed it. As a consequence of the failure of political leadership to build a consensus over the question of federal design, the CA was expired without giving a birth to the new constitution.

The purpose of transferring Nepal into a federal state is, as outlined in its Interim Constitution 2007, to end discrimination based on caste/ethnicity, language, culture, religion, region and others (gender and class). This somehow provides a guideline for constituting provinces as federal units. The Committee of State Restructuring and Distribution of State Power (CSRDSP), a thematic committee of the CA which was assigned to craft a federal Nepal, had adopted identity as primary factor and capability as secondary, while recommending 14 provinces[1] for federal Nepal. The identity is shaped by a combination of five aspects: (1) caste/ethnicity/ community (2) language (3) culture (4) geographical/territorial continuity (in settlement of targeted groups) and (5) historical continuity (in settlement of targeted groups). Capability is an aggregation of four variables: (1) economic interrelations and existing capability (2) present state of or potentiality for infrastructural development (3) availability of natural resources and (4) administrative accessibility. There are many dissenting opinions against the CSRDSP's preliminary draft of federal

---

1   The proposed 14 provinces are: Limbuwan, Kirat, Sherpa, Mithila-Bhojpur-Koch Madhes, Tamsaling, Sunkoshi, Newa, Narayani, Tamuwan, Magarat, Lumbini-Awad-Tharuwan, Karnali, Khaptad and Jadan.

design that surfaced within and outside the CA.

Assuming that differences of opinion on the CSRDSP's proposal could be solved through making a revision and refinement, a High Level State Restructuring Recommendation Commission (HLSRRC) was formed in November 2011. The HLSRRC uphold the principles adopted by the CSRDSP. But taking into account the public criticism that the CSRDSP ignored capability factor, the HLSRRC tried its best to balance both capability and identity factors and so it adopted 'identity with capability' as the main bases for the creation of provinces. Some proposed provinces (by CSRDSP) i.e. Sherpa, Sunkoshi and Jadan were taken out from the frame on account of non-viability and Karnali and Khaptad was merged into one single province. The HLSRRC also considered the public opinions for reduction of the number of provinces and voice against the ethnic contents on the proposed federalism. It, therefore, made two major revisions on the CSRDSP's original proposals: one reducing the number of provinces into 10^2, and the other, taking out the provision of *agradhikar* (preferential rights) of the targeted group to the post of chief executive of the province. On territorial boundary of province, the HLSRRC gave emphasis in making the province demographically convenient to the targeted group. Despite its contribution in some aspects – reduction of number of provinces and rejection of the provision of *agradhikar* – was appreciated, the HLSRRC's recommendation did not help to resolve overall problems; it rather contributed to intensify divergences of opinions on several issues, i.e. name of provinces, number of provinces, delineation of provincial boundary, division of power between centre and province, minority rights, nature and scope of autonomy and rights to self determination etc. Above all, primacy of identity for making constituent units has continued to remain as the most contentious and controversial issue. Nepali society and politics is divided between ones who want to keep primacy of identity as the main factor and others who argue to place capability as the topmost important factor.

Ethnic Upsurge

The post-1990 democracy period stands witness ethnic upsurge (Bhattachan, 2000; Hachhethu, 2003; Hangen, 2010). Nepal is a part of

2   The HLSRRC proposed 10 provinces are: Limbuwan, Kirat, Madhesh- Mithila-Bhojpur, Tamsaling, Newa, Narayani, Tamuwan, Magarat, Madhesh- Awad-Tharuwan, and Karnali and Khaptad.

global phenomenon of ethnic upheavals accompanying with the third wave of democracy. Out of 110 major armed conflicts recorded in a period between 1989 and 1999, 103 took place within existing states, mostly focused around identity issues (Quoted in Reilly 2001: 2). Nepal is still exempted from ethnic war if the ethnic content of the Maoist insurgency and sporadic armed rides in Madhesh are not counted. Inter-ethnic relation in Nepal largely appears none-antagonistic, so, some see it as harmonious and free of violence (Sharma, 1997; Dahal, 1995; Pradhan, 2002). This is but not substantiated by micro level studies, - i.e. Caplan's research in east hill (1970), Gaige's study on Madhesh (1975) etc. Thus, "The ethnic harmony may have been exaggerated" (Gellener, 1997: 6) and, to the extreme, it is "blatantly manufactured myth" (Bhattachan, 1995: 125). Over the time, ethnic relation has been changing rapidly towards the greater degree of discord, conflict and tension since the rise of ethnic movements in aftermath of the restoration of democracy in 1990. On emergence of ethnicity and regionalism as a dominant part of the Nepali polity, a foreign expert on Nepali society and politics observed "If the period 1960 to 1990 was one of nation-building, the 17 years since then has been a time of ethnicity-building" (Gellner 2007: 1823).

Some major notable agencies which have contributed for making ethnicity as one of the dominant parts of contemporary Nepal are: (a) Nepal Federation of Indigenous Nationalities (NEFIN, a platform of 54 ethnic organizations) (b) Madhesh based regional political parties (c) CPN-Maoist, a largest party of the CA which has blended ethnic rights and class ideology since the time of its insurgency and (d) international conventions (ILO 169 and UN Declaration of Rights of Indigenous Nationalities in particular) and international communities which have contributed to linking local initiatives as a part of the global movement. Over time, Nepali state and political parties have gradually become receptive to the cause of excluded groups, accommodating them, although only a token accommodation, in public domain, in party apparatus and amplifying party policy platforms related to ethnic issues with each successive parliamentary election in the 1990s (Hachhethu, 2003b).

The accumulative effect of politicization of ethnicity from different platforms is quite visible both in bottom-up movement and top-down policy. Census data reveals disassociation with Hindu religion and Nepali language as their population decreased from 87 percent in 1991 to 80 percent in 2001 and from 52 percent in 1991 to 48 percent in 2001 respectively. Such a trend of differentiate with Hindu religion and Nepali language is likely to increase in the recent census of 2011. To be a non-Hindu by origin is one of the qualifications of being Janajanti, according to NEFIN definition. Surveys findings (conducted over a period of three years, first in 2004 and the second in 2007) show that people's preference to ethnic/regional identity is on rise and identification with national identity is down, from 58 to 43 per cent. (Hachhethu 2004; Hachhethu et al 2008).

In past, nation building elsewhere in the world was tantamount to ethnicity destroying. European model of nation building prescribed an imposition of a majority group's language and culture on the rest of the population. On how the minorities of the West had become victim of such a model of creating modern nation-state, Kymlicka explains, "Various efforts were made to erode this sense of distinct nationhood, including restricting minority language rights, abolishing traditional forms of local or regional self-government and encouraging members of the dominant group to settle in the minority group's traditional territory so that the minority becomes outnumbered even in its traditional territory" (2006: 33). Most third world countries followed their colonial master's framework of nation building for the post-independence time. On the case of South Asian countries, Phandis and Ganjuli states, "...post-colonial nation building approaches focused almost exclusively on creating a unified 'national identity' based around either common political values and citizenship or a putative majoritarian ethnic identity" (2001: 13). Nepali model of national integration, as adopted till the recent past, tells the similar story of homogenisation and assimilation of diverse groups into the fold of the majority group's culture.

Since the time of unification of Nepal, the rulers – Shahs (1768-1846), Ranas (1846-1951), Panchas (1960;1990), and political parties (1990 onwards) – had tried to develop Nepal as a homogeneous, monolithic and unitary state providing protection to one language (Nepali), one caste group (hill Bahun-Chhetri), and one religion (Hindu), ignoring the reality of diversified and pluralistic character of the Nepali society. It was, therefore, an "empire model" of national integration (Pfaff-Czarnecka, 1997: 421). Since the Nepali state had long "functioned as an ethnicity based exploitative state" (Riaz and Basu, 2010: 80), territorial unification did not follow national integration in a way of multicultural nationalism

(Gurung, 1998; 2001). Besides, the state-designed 'Nepalization' process – through Hinduisation, spread of the Parbatiya's culture, institutionalization of caste system converting separate identity of ethnic groups into caste structures, and centralization of politics and administration – had led to increase disparity among different social groups. The hill high caste Brahmin-Chhetri and Newar have long been in privileged position. Other groups, i.e. Janajati, Madhesi and Dalit are generally marginalized. The legacy of history is well reflected in unequal distribution of socio-economic resources of the country and in representation of political power structure of the country.

Ethnic tension in many multicultural states is rooted with inequality of social groups (Duchacek 1970; Mallick 1999; Ghai, 2011). Flenier et all list out six factors that stimulated for ethnic conflicts, these are: economic injustice, past discrimination, suppression of minority culture, lack of trust of minority groups to the state, cross-national ethnic affinity, and unscrupulous manipulation by warlords (2003:202). Nepal is also a case that explains that social inequality, deprivation and discrimination produce a politics of ethnic identity.

Nepal: Human Development Report (1998) and *Unequal Citizens* (2006) are two among several other scholarly works that provide an intellectual foundation for ethnic movement as these publications give an empirical and statistical evidences of inequality among the social groups of Nepal. Nepali society is largely organized in stratified hierarchical order in which Brahmin and Chhetri place at the top, Janajati in the middle and Dalit at the lowest position. The superior position of hill high castes correspondences to their better of position in human development index whereas the Janajati and Madheshi (except Newar and plains high castes respectively) fall into category of excluded and marginalized groups. Figure of hill castes Brahim/Chhetri on poverty index is much lower (18 percent) than national average of 31 percent whereas for the rest other groups people under below poverty line is much higher. The dominant and marginalized paradigm between hill high castes and other social groups is also well reflected in distribution of political power structure of the country. The hill high castes constitute only 30 percent of the total population of the country but their dominance in the state power is 66 percent. The scenario is just the opposite as far as other groups are concerned with the exception of Newar (among Janajatis) and some high caste people from the Madhesis (Bahun, Bhumihar, Kayastha and Rajput). Against this background, the recent ethnic identity movements have increasingly been accelerated aiming to end domination of hill high castes. "The new politics of identity and recognition is seen as emancipatory and empowering of the hitherto marginalized and oppressed communities; it is the weapon of the weak, redressing past injustice; and enriches society through diversity" (Ghai, 2011: 315). In retrospect, the inequality between dominant group (hill Bahau/Chhetri) and minority group (Madheshi, Janajati and Dalit) is byproduct of the legacy of the historical process of national integration in Nepal.

Modernization – though it, in the beginning, tended to achieve homogeneous nation-state for multicultural society – eventually produces politics of ethnic identity. A number of empirical studies, i.e. Gurr on Africa (1993, quoted in Kymlicka) and Weiner on India (1978) reveal that groups' competition rather than groups' inequalities produces ethnic conflicts. Indian story, as explored by Weiner, tells that "… middle class nativist movements in opposition to migrants tend to emerge in those communities where the local population has recently produced its own educated class that aspires to move into jobs held by migrants (Weiner, 1978: 8). For Chaitanya Mishra, Nepal's case is not different from other countries' experiences as he asserts that "…competition for non rural and nonagricultural sources of living… is the space where the ethnic and other struggle is being waged in (2011: 24). Going back to generalization of competition and ethnicity, Brass's thought could be referred here, "Ethnic identity formation is viewed as a process that involves three sets of struggles, struggle for control over material and symbolic resources, competition for rights, privileges and available resources, and for or against domination on given national or sub-national territory. (1991: 247). In the Nepali context, the moot question is did the post-1990 democracy provide political and constitutional arrangements for fair competition among the unequal social groups. The problem is, from the perspective of multiculturalism, not inequality among the individual citizens of the country but inequality between social groups. The notion of multiculturalism suggests group equality in public domain. It seeks equality for diverse cultures (Mahajan, 2002: 19).

The 1990 Constitution – promulgated against the background of the fall of three decade long authoritarian party less panchayat system and restoration of multiparty system – adopted the ethos of liberal democracy. Theoretically speaking, classical democratic model denies constitutional recognition to distinct communities as bearer of rights (Haysam, 2003; Smith 2000). This was well reflected in Nepali politics under second experiment of democracy (1990-2006). The 1990 Constitution recognized pluralistic character of Nepali society consisting of diverse cultural and linguistic groups. The constitutional provisions to "maintain cultural diversity", right "to promote literature, scripts, arts and culture of different groups", freedom "to protect religious places and trust" and recognition of other than Nepali (language of the nation) as "languages of nationalities" were certainly new contents which were not found in previous constitutions. But, the post-1990 party system, because of its over utterance to the principle of individual rights of citizen, ignored the significance of collective rights and so the constitutional designation of Nepal as a 'multi-ethnic and multi-lingual state' lacked any substantial policy and programme to address the problems of the excluded groups. Moreover, competitive politics in line with caste, ethnicity, language, and region was prohibited constitutionally. As the 1990 Constitution recognized Nepal as a unitary, Hindu, and monarchical state, and Nepali as official language as before, many things remained unchanged in the basic characteristics of Nepali state. National symbols – crown, scepter, royal crest, royal standard, coat-of arms, cow, national flag, rhododendron, and red blob – set by Panchayat and most of them associated with monarchy and Hindu religion (Gurung, 1997: 505) and national anthem (phrased in a way equating patriotism with worship to king) retained without any change. So the post-1990 democracy "... established or more accurately endorsed the exclusionary nature of the state" (Ghai, 2011: 310). With acknowledgment to the limitation of liberal democracy to address the problems of multiethnic states, Lawati concludes that Westminster model is unsuitable to pluralistic society of Nepal (2005). In retrospect, negligence to the pluralism under democratic dispensation provided a ground for the assertion of ethnic identity and accommodation.

Management of Diversity and Conflicts

Nepali state, in aftermath of a successful popular uprising of April 2006, has changed its role substantially from its acts of pursuing ethnic decline in the past (at time a policy of national integration through assimilation was adopted) into its responses for ethnic formation. Such a reversal role of the state in the West has become possible because of "desecuritization of state-minority relations and the cross-ethnic consensus on liberal democratic values" (Kymlicka, 2006: 41). The context of Nepal for a dramatic change of state's image from that of exclusionary to inclusive is different. Nepal state is not catalyst rather a receptive of pressures for state restructuring project. Weakened by a decade long civil war (1996-2006) and erosion of legitimacy of mainstream parties, Nepal state failed to resist wave of rising ethnic and regional aspirations and movements. The ethnic movement in post-April 2006 *Jana Andolan* II geared up from a quest for identity to pressure for power sharing. Ethnic demands can broadly be classified into three categories: identity, sharing of resources, and representation in state apparatus.

Nepali state and government in the post-April 2006 popular uprising, dominated by the eight parties including the CPN-Maoist, appeared liberal on issues related to identity question converting Nepal from Hindu to secular state and recognizing a need of bi/multi language policy for the future. But it failed to preempt, in the early phase of transition, to ethnic and regional aspiration of power sharing. So, the promulgation of the Interim Constitution 2007 added a new dimension to transitional politics. It sparked a battle for inclusive democracy by various social forces who felt that their interests had not been represented in the Interim Constitution. The Madhesh uprising of January-February 2007 was powerful in terms of popular participation and its impact. During this 21-day long violent movement participated in by large masses of people of plains origin, 27 people lost their lives, compared to 21 in the April 2006 uprising. Connected to the Madhesh uprising was the tragic massacre of 27 Maoists in Rautahat, a tarai district. The Madhesh uprising brought the transitional authority in favour of inclusive democracy. A lot of agreements, made between the then interim transitional government and different ethnic groups, centered on advancing Nepal into an inclusive democracy.

No doubt, Nepal, in aftermath of the April 2006 popular uprising, is heading towards a new destination that is close to the model of consociational democracy. Four cornerstones of consociationalism are: grand coalition government with representation of major social groups, proportional representation of different groups in legislature and administration, segmental autonomy via federalism or similar devise, and a power of veto over key decisions by minority groups (Lijphart, 1977). Management of identity politics in Nepal is explained in following sections.

As the phrase 'unity in diversity' has been (ab)used for imposition of dominant culture in Nepal, the country should move ahead in spirit with 'live in diversity with unity'. A combination of unity and diversity as a means of management of ethnic conflicts demands tolerance, reconciliation, enhancement of diversity and equalization of majorities and minorities (Flenier et al, 2003: 203-207). Furthermore, recognition of diverse identities in multiethnic societies includes (a) protection and promotion of cultural, economic and political rights of disadvantaged minorities (b) recognition of ethno-political claims (c) power sharing arrangement at the centre among politically organized social groups and (d) power devolution to the peoples who are regionally concentrated (Gurr, 1997: 13). It requires a revision on the major principle of liberal democracy ensuring equality among the ethnic groups and within an ethnic group. Some concrete decisions regarding recognition of diverse identities that made in aftermath of the post-April 2006 popular uprising which were incorporated in the Interim Constitution 2007 are: (a) declaration of Nepal as a secular state, (b) recognition of all languages existing in Nepal as national languages, (c) reservation of 45 percent in the civil service for underprivileged sections of society, (d) affirmative actions to marginalized groups, (e) declaration of Nepal as a federal state, and (f) provision of proportional representation of social groups in proportion to size of their own population for the election of the CA.

The CA of Nepal, in terms of caste/ethnic backgrounds of its members, was a reflective body of social mosaic of the country. It has become possible because of adaptation of inclusive representation system. In fact, consociationalism believes that the electoral system is the most powerful instrument of shaping the political system, majoritarian or consociational. Lewis' argues that divided societies need proportional representation to give minorities adequate representation, discouraging parochialism, and force moderation of the political parties (quoted in Reilly, 2001: 20). For inclusive representation of ethnic groups in state apparatus, African states have adopted a wide verity of different mechanisms, i.e. proportional representation (South Africa, Namibia, Lesotho), requirement of support of ethno-regional provinces for the election of the President (Nigeria), rights of opposition parties to participate in cabinet (South Africa, Zimbabwe), making Upper Chamber as House of Nationalities (Ethiopia, Uganda, Burundi), ethnic distribution to highest post of court and administration (Nigeria, South Africa) etc (Haysom, 2003: 207). Indian political system is also advancing with inclusive attributes, i.e. creation of federal units on the basis of language, constitutional provisions for reservation to backward sections of the people and reserved seats to the schedule castes and schedule tribes in elected houses at national, provincial and local level. Nepal, for the election to the CA, adopted a mixed parallel system (FPTP and PR) giving a greater weight to the PR, 56 percent or 335 out of total 601 seats. Seats allocated for the FPTP was 240 (40 percent). For those elected from the PR system, the contesting parties must ensure representation of different social groups in proportion as follows: 37 percent for Janajati, 31 percent for Madheshis, 13 percent for Dalits, 4 percent for backward region, and 30 percent for others (hill Brahmin, Chhetri, Thakuri and Sanyasi). Besides, NEFIN successfully negotiated in placing Janajatis (which left out from representation from FPTP or PR) as beneficiaries in 26 seats allocated to the Cabinet's nomination. Similarly Madheshi also succeeded in inserting a provision that parties contesting less than 30 percent seats were exempted from the provision of inclusive candidacy under the PR system. Consequently, Janajati and Madheshis along with other excluded groups received a greater share in the CA against their under-representation in national legislature in the past.

The CA election was credited for power shift in regards to social makes up of political power structure. Looking through the caste/ethnic composition, the CA could be said a departure from the past as the faces of the hill Hindu high castes, Brahmin and Chhetri, reduced substantially from 56-63 percent in the House of Representatives (HOR) of the 1990s into 33 percent in the CA, only 3 percent higher than their strength of population (30 percent). For the first time in the history of Nepal, the Madheshis (including caste, ethnic, Dalit and Muslim) gained a higher representation (34 percent) than its population size (31 percent) against the past record of their representation by only around 20 percent. The Janajatis (of both hill and tarai) had also strength of 35 percent – though it is 2 percent lower than their population size (37 percent) – which is significant as its representation in the past was around 25 percent. Representation of Dalits also increased from less than 1 percent to 8 percent. Having one third women in the CA was also a new phenomenon. The CA elections along with the constitutional provision of caste/ethnic based representation for 56 percent seats (allocated under PR system) of total 601 members of the CA, provided an outlet for translating identity movement into political power.

Restructuring Nepali state into a federal form is not a project initiated by the state; it is rather an outcome of Janajati and Madheshi movements. These groups have, therefore, a lot of hope and expectation of getting due share in political power structure of the county under federal design. As federalism provides a political mechanism for self rule and autonomy, it is seen as a solution to the long standing unitary, exclusionary and patrimonial characters of Nepali state (Riaz and Basu, 2010: 80; Lama, 2008: 115). The quest for federalism is significant in advancing democracy in Nepal from that of conventional plebiscite structure to inclusive governance. Federal state, by any standard, is more inclusive than unitary one. As division of power on territory basis is the core of federalism, it naturally provides greater space to the minorities in sharing of social, economic and political power of the country.

Theoretically speaking and empirically proven fact is that federalism is attracted for three major reasons. One, it gives ethnicity a overwhelming importance which means federalism serves as a means of accommodating ethnic diversity and minimizing conflicts (Turton, 2006; Suberu, 2006; Roy, 2006; Ilago et al, 2006; Blendenbacher, 2003; Thurer, 2006). Two, it celebrates variety and creates unity out of diversity (Sadik, 2003; Fleiner et al, 2006) hence it reduces likelihood of secession (Kymlicka, 2006; Montes, 2006). While speaking about India, Bharagava states, "… that the democratic and linguistic federalism of India has managed to combine legitimate claims of national unity with equally legitimate claims of the political recognition of relatively distinct cultural groups" (2006: 93). Three, it offers consensus democracy against majoritarian democracy (Montes, 2006: 161). In addition, federalism allows losers at national political level to be winner at the sub-national or local level (Haysom, 2003: 227). For multiple advantages that federalism offers, a scholar of this subjects highlights:

"The combination of unity and diversity that federalism offers potentially enables a multicultural society to have its cake and eat too. It enables minorities to become majorities in sub-national units thus assisting to answer the question "who should govern whom?" It provides a means for recognition and acceptance of different languages, religions and cultures. Most importantly of all, perhaps, it embraces diversity, it positively values diversity, it can promote diversity, and thus can capture the benefits of diversity. In this way

it increases the legitimacy of state in the eyes and hearts of its entire people and not merely of a dominant group. In societies in conflict or potential conflict, this has the further advantage of increasing the likelihood that a real peace will be made and will hold" (Saunders, 2003: 34).

In responding to recent successful and aggressive ethnic identity movement, Nepali state has changed its role from that of ethnicity decline in the past to ethnicity building at present. It opens up a vista of restructuring the state as a mechanism of management of ethnic conflict between traditionally dominant group and historically marginalized groups on the one hand. It, on the other hand, also produces new form of ethnic conflicts. At the moment the ethnic conflicts center around the question of what type of federalism Nepal should have. Clash of interest among different social groups appear on number of issues, particularly on name, number and boundary of provinces.

Differences of opinion emerged between ones which are committed federalists and others which accept federal design reluctantly. Madhesh based parties were founded with federal agenda. The CPN-Maoist has advanced its position from its initial proposal of autonomous regions (resemble of Chinese model) into federalism with multiparty competitive system. Most political parties including the NC and UML have been dragged into federal idea later. The establishment of inclusive democracy through federalism means ending the dominance of hill high caste people in state power (Hachhethu et al 2008). Thus, federalism is not a natural choice for hill caste groups. It is also not unnatural to have its effect in political parties because hill Bahuns are at the helm of most of the country's political parties. Federalism is also not the first choice of most of the major mainstream political parties. It is, however, a good choice for other communities of Nepali society such as Janajatis and Madhesis. The establishment of a federal Nepal would be a good way of addressing the common aspirations and wishes of nearly two-thirds of the total population of the country, who are seeking social identity, political representation and economic development.

Nevertheless, a debate about whether Nepal should transfer into federal path or not is gone issue. The dominant question is: what type of federalism suits to Nepal? The Nepali society and politics is divided on this issue. Divergences among the communities matter more than disagreement among the political parties. Three major stakeholder social groups having conflicting interest and different approaches are: Khas-Arya, Janajati and Madheshi. There is in-party polarization along the caste/ethnic and regional lines in each of major and minor political parties. The indigenous people are in favor of ethnic federalism; while the Madheshis favor regional (ecological) identity based federalism; and hill caste people are in favor of provinces created by combining mountain, hill and tarai and preserving existing administrative territory and demography.

Both Janajati and Madheshi are championing for one or other form of ethnic federalism. Demand of ethnic autonomy precedes the declaration of Nepal as a federal state. Ethnic/regional autonomous province with the right to self-determination was heard loudly during the Janajati and Madhesh movements. Janajatis have frequently refereed international conventions like ILO 169 and the UN Declaration on the Rights of Indigenous Nationalities 2007 while claiming right of endogenous people on *jal, jangal* and *jamin* (water, forest and land). The Madheshis have also taken this point but in different way, asserting for their 'first right' in the natural resources of plains areas spreading into 20 tarai district. Federalism means – what the masses of Janajati and Madheshi understand or what they want to convey – is a system that blends 'share rule' at centre and 'self rule' at province. As they are thinking the disaggregation of boundary of federal units on the bases of ethnicity, the present disadvantage groups – Madheshi and Janajati in particular – is hoping to get double benefit: domination in their respective province and a sharing the power of the central government/administration. For them, the minimal definition of autonomy and right to self determination is making 'strong province', otherwise, some interpret it to the extent of right to secede.

The idea of making ethnic federalism obviously hurts the hill castes' sentiment and interest. The Bahun and Chhetri ethnicity has recently emerged to counter the demands of ethnic federalism. They are trying their best to minimize ethnic contents of Nepali federalism so arguing to use non-ethnic name of provinces, to reduce the number of provinces, and to avoid preferential rights of disadvantaged ethnic groups.

Ethnic conflict between the hill castes and Janajati and Madheshi is distinct over the issue of federal design in Nepal. Solutions of many problems lay on the proposal of the CSRDSP (a thematic committee of the CA which is assigned to craft federal Nepal) and recommendation made by the HLSRRC. The Committee and the Commission did not go to the extent of ethnic federalism though their reports entertained a number of ethnic contents, i.e. ethnic name of provinces, autonomous regions for tiny Janajatis, reinvention of cultural territory while delineating provinces' boundary. Unlike Ethiopia, Nigeria, Bosnia-Herzegovina and Belgium all known as countries of ethnic federalism, the CSRDSP did not subscribe ethnic group as constituent units. So far ethnic preference rights is concerned, a proposal of *agradhikar* to the targeted ethnic group to the chief executive post of province for the first two tenures is exception. It is but rejected by the HLSRRC. So both the Committee and the Commission did not provide constitutional arrangement for discrimination against any groups, be they dominant or deprived in the present power structure of the country. For instance, the right to self-determination, limited in a way which will not allow secession, is granted to indigenous groups (to Khas-Arya by implication), indigenous Janajati and Madhesis. These words (indigenous groups, indigenous Janajati and Madhesis) cover almost all the communities or groups of Nepal. Similarly, first right on natural resources are provided not only to indigenous Janajati but also to the local community. Along with local language (a mother tongue of the targeted ethnic group), Nepali (mother tongue of Khas-Arya) is retained as a medium of education and official language at sub-national and local level.

Potential Ethnic Conflicts under Federal Nepal

There is no doubt that federal Nepal comes up with some new conflicts and it also paves the way to intensify some other existing conflicts. Three major conflicts can be anticipated.

One, a longstanding conflict between hill high castes and ethnic groups and between Pahadi and Madhshi at macro level is likely to shift into inter-groups competition at sub-national level. Most provinces proposed by the CSRDSP and the HLSRRC are multiethnic. Caste/ethnic breakdown of human geography of the HLSRRC's proposed 10 provinces suggests three categories of federal units: (1) provinces with the presence of targeted group as the majority population (Mithila-Bhojpura-Koch Madhesh, Narayani, and Khaptad-Karnali) (2) provinces in which the targeted groups constitute as dominant groups (Limbuwan, Kirat, Tamshaling, Magarat and Madhesh-Abadh-Tharuwan), and (3) provinces that targeted groups are in minority with small margin of less than one percent vis-à-vis hill high castes (Newa and Tamuwan). As stated above that the HLSRRC gave emphasis to the creation of demographically convenient provinces despite most of its recommended provinces are multicultural. In such a situation there will be no need for political preferential right. Generally, a multicultural province suffers from ethnic conflicts if the provision of preferential rights is granted to one group against others.

Two, there is risk of discrimination by the majority group at province level against the minorities. Preference right to hitherto the disadvantaged sections of society is considered as an essential tool to achieve group equality. But the problems is vesting such rights to the dominant group of province and dividing the people in line between 'sons of the soil' and 'outsiders'. In India – a country considered as non-ethnic federal because of having accommodative and pluralistic politics at the Centre, many of the state governments have provided preferential rights to the 'sons of the soil' pursuing discriminatory policies towards their internal minorities (Weiner, 1978; Bhargava, 2006). Nigeria is an extreme example that the concept of 'indigene' is manipulated to perpetuate discriminatory practices that exclude non-indigenes from opportunities, controlled by the sub-national government. Non-indigenes are discriminated against and denied access to economic, political and social privileges (Suberu 2006: 79; Galadima, 2010: 69). For Nepal, constitutional arrangement as per recommendation by the CSRDSP and the HLSRRC is likely to be modest in this regard. For provincial administration, they suggested a provision of preference right not in ethnic line rather on territory basis. However, one can not rule out the possibility that the provincial politics may push the government to act favouring the dominant group in practice if not in legal provision. Preference rights with or without constitutional/legal provision will become another source of conflicts.

Three, intra-ethnic conflict is likely to intensify. At time federalism begins to work, intra-ethnic conflict is likely to come into the fore. At the outset, there is indication. The provision of ethnic preferential rights to the chief executive post is opposed not only by hill castes but also by those Janajatis who are going to be excluded from this benefit. The idea of making Limbu as only eligible to become Chief Minister in Limbuwan is unacceptable to other Janajatis, i.e Rai, Newar, Gurung etc living in that province. Though all Janajatis are united vertically to fighting against the hill castes domination, they are not a cohesive unit. The dynamic of provincial politics may invite a horizontal conflict at sub-national level between the dominant Janajati and minority Janajatis. Madheshis – a common tag used to peoples of non-hill origin – are also divided into three distinct groups, Hindu versus Muslim, castes versus ethnic groups, and forwards versus backwards. The day-to-day life of Madhesh is affected more by internal division of Madheshis themselves. The component of heterogeneity and divergence is much deeper among the Madheshis than Janajatis. Cultural differences between the Madheshi Janajatis and the Madheshi caste groups are as large as those between the hill castes and the hill Janajati groups. Divergence among the non-hill origin people and distinction of one against another group is further evident from the fact that Tharu and Muslim feel uncomfortable in living with Madheshi identity.

Conclusion

Restructuring the Nepali state with inclusive polity and federal design is acclaimed, particularly by Janajatis and Madheshis, as a remedy of longstanding ethnic problems of the country. But if the federal Nepal is not crafted well and managed properly, it could also be a journey towards a danger zone. No doubt, federal Nepal under designing should address the problem of exclusion; it, at the same time, should be accommodative to different and conflicting interest of diverse social groups so that people belonging to different segments of society could feel a sense of their ownership on new federal Nepal. The structure of federal Nepal should be in line with some elements of consociasonal democracy. Taking into account multicultural character of most provinces, consocionalism should be rule of the game not only at national level but also at province level. Here, some recommendations made by the CSRDSP and the HLSRRC are noteworthy, i.e. inclusive representation of different social groups (at both national and province level) in proportion to size of their own population, preferential rights or positive discrimination for excluded groups i.e. Dalits, women, tiny ethnic minorities, not to the dominant group of the province, retention of Nepali language along with recognition of local language as medium of education and official language at province level, prime rights vests to indigenous people as well as local community etc. Capacity of national political parties to balance between claims and counter claims and also the ability of ethnic or regional parties to foster a harmonious politics count a lot. Besides, Nepal needs to build a federal culture with tolerance, compromise and respect to diversities.

References

Bhattachan, Krishna Bahadur. 1995. "Ethnopolitics and Ethnodevelopment: An Emerging Paradigm". In Dhruba Kumar (ed.) *State, Leadership and Politics in Nepal*. Kathmandu: CNAS.

-- -- --. 2000. "Possible Ethnic Revolution Or Insurgency in a Predatory Unitary Hindu State, Nepal". In Dhruba Kumar (ed.) *Domestic Conflict and Crisis of Governability in Nepal*. Kathmandu: CNAS.

Bhargava, Rajiv. 2006. "The Evolution and Distinctiveness of India's Linguistic Federalism". In David Turton (ed.). *Ethnic Federalism*. Oxford: James Currey Ltd. 93-118.

Blendenbacher, Raoul and Ronald L. Watts. 2003. "Federalism in a Changing World: A Conceptual Framework for the Conference". In Raoul Blendenbacher and Arnold Koller (eds.) *Federalism in a Changing World*. London: McGill-Queen's University Press. 7-25.

Brass, Paul. R. 1991. *Ethnicity and Nationalism: Theory and Comparison*. New Delhi: Sage.

Caplan, Lionel. 1970, *Land and Social Change in East Nepal: A Study of Hindu-tribal relations*. London: Routledge and Kegan Paul Limited.

CBS. 2002. *Population Census 2001*, Kathmandu: Central Bureau of Statistics.

Dahal, Dilli Ram. 1995. "Ethnic Cauldron, Demography and Minority Politics: The Case of Nepal." In Dhruba Kumar (ed.) *State, Leadership and Politics in Nepal*. Kathmandu: Centre for Nepal and Asian Studies (CNAS).

DFID and the World Bank. 2006. *Unequal Citizens*. Kathmandu: DFID and the World Bank.

Duchacek, Ivo. D. 1970. *Comparative Federalism: The Territorial Dimension of Politics*. New Work: Holt, Rinhart and Winston Inc.

Election Commission. 2008. *Result of the 2008 Constituent Assembly Election*. Kathmandu: Election Commission.

Fleiner, Thomas et al. 2003. "Federalism, Decentralization and Conflict

Management in Multicultural Societies". In Raoul Blendenbacher and Arnold Koller (eds.) *Federalism in a Changing World*. London: McGill-Queen's University Press. London: McGill-Queen's University Press. 297-215.

Gaige, Frederick H. 1975. *Regionalism and National Unity in Nepal*. Delhi: Vikas Publishing House.

Galadima, Habu S. 2010. "Nigeria: A Developing Federation under Strains". *Indian Journal of Federal Studies*. V.1. 59-74.

Gellner, David N. 1997. "Ethnicity and Nationalism in the World's only Hindu State". In David N. Gellner et al (eds.). *Nationalism and Ethnicity in a Hindu Kingdom: The Politics of Culture in Contemporary Nepal*. Amsterdam: Harwood Academic Publishers.

-- -- --. "Caste, Ethnicity and Inequality in Nepal". *Economic and Political Weekly*. XLLII:20.

Ghai, Yash. 2011. "Ethnic Identity, Participation and Social Justice: A Constitution for New Nepal?. *International Journal of Minority and Group Rights*. N.18. 309-334.

Gurr, Ted Robert. 1997. "Why do Minorities Rebel? The Worldwide Geography of Ethnopolitical Conflicts". In Gunther Bachier (ed.) *Federalism against Ethnicity?*. Zurich: Verlag Ruegger AG.

Gurung, Harka. 1997. "State and Society in Nepal". In David N. Gellner Jonna Pfaff-Czarnecka, and John Whelpton (eds.) *Nationalism and Ethnicity in a Hindu Kingdom: The Politics of Culture in Contemporary Nepal*. Amsterdam: Harwood academic publishers pp. 495- 532.

-- -- --. 1998. *Nepal: social Demography and Expressions*. Kathmandu: New Era.

-- -- --. 2001. "Nepali Nationalism: A Matter of Consolidation". *Himal*. 14:3, pp. 18-22.

Hachhethu, Krishna. 2002. *Party Building in Nepal: Organization, Leadership and People*, Kathmandu: Mandala Book Point.

-- -- --. 2009. *State Building in Nepal: Creating a Functional State*.

Kathmandu:ESP.

-- -- --.2003. "Democracy and Nationalism: Interface between State and Ethnicity in Nepal". *Contributions to Nepalese Studies*. 30: 2. 217-252.

-- -- --. 2003 (b). "Nepal: Party Manifesto and Election". *Nepali Journal of Contemporary Studies*, 3:1. 21-50.

-- -- --. 2004. *State of Democracy in Nepal: Survey Report*, Kathmandu: SDSA/N and International IDEA.

Hachhethu, Krishna et al. 2008. *Nepal in Transition: A Study on the State of Democracy*, Stockholm: International IDEA.

Hangen, Susan I. 2010. *The Rise of Ethnic Politics in Nepal: Democracy in the Margins*. London: Routledge.

Hayssom, Nicholas R.L. 2003. "Constitution Making and Nationa Building". In Raoul Blendenbacher and Arnold Koller (eds.) *Federalism in a Changing World*. London: McGill-Queen's University Press. 216-239.

Interim Constitution of Nepal 2007.

Ilago, Simeon Augustin et al. 2006. "Shattering Myths and Affirming Facts" in Simeon Augustin Ilago and Raphael N. Montes (eds.) *Federalism and Multiculturalism*. Manila: Centre for Local and Regional Governance. 139-154.

Kymlicka, Will. 2006. "Emerging Western Models of Multination Federalism". In David Turton (ed.). *Ethnic Federalism*. Oxford: James Currey Ltd. 32-64.

Lama, Mukta Singh. 2008. "Samanta, Sanghiyata ra Bahusanskritik Rastrabad" (Equality, Federalism and Multicultural Nationalism". In Krishna P. Khanal, Jhalak Subedi and Mukta Singh Lama, *Rajyako Punasanrachana: Rajnitik, Arthik ra Sanskritik Dristikon* (State Restructuring: Political, Economic and Cultural Perspectives), Kathmandu: Martin Choutari.

Lawati, Mahendra. 2005. *Towards a Democratic Nepal: Inclusive Political Institutions for a Multicultural Society*. Kathmandu: Mandala Book

Point.

Lijphart, Arend. 1977. *Democracy in Plural Societies: A Comparative Exploration.* London: Yale University Press.

Mahajan, Gurpreet. 2002. *The Multicultural Path: Issues of Diversity and Discrimination in Democracy.* New Delhi: Sage.

Mallick, Ross. 1998. *Development, Ethnicity and Human Rights in South Asia.* New Delhi: Sage.

Mishra, Chaitanya. 2004. "Ethnic Upsurge in Nepal: Implications for Federalization". (unpublished paper)

Montes, Raphel N. 2006. "Understanding Federalism". In Simeon Augustin Ilago and Raphael N. Montes (eds.) *Federalism and Multiculturalism.* Manila: Centre for Local and Regional Governance. 157-176.

NESAC. 1998. *Nepal: Human Development Report 1998.* Kathmandu: Nepal South Asia Centre.

Neupane, Govinda. 2000. *Nepalko Jatiya Prasana* (Question of Caste/ Ethnicity in Nepal). Kathmandu: Centre for Development Studies.

Pfaff-Czarnecka, Jonna. 1997. "Vestiges and Visions: Cultural Change in the Process of Nation-Building in Nepal". In David N. Gellner Jonna Pfaff-Czarnecka, and John Whelpton (eds.) *Nationalism and Ethnicity in a Hindu Kingdom: The Politics of Culture in Contemporary Nepal.* Amsterdam: Harwood academic publishers pp. 419-470.

Phandis, Urmila and Rajat Gaunguly. 2001. *Ethnicity and Nation Building in South Asia.* New Delhi: Sage Publications.

Pradhan, Rajendra. 2002. "Ethnicity, Caste and Pluralistic Society". In Kanak Mani Dixit and Shastri Ramachandran. *State of Nepal.* Kathmandu: Himal Books, pp. 1-21.

Reilly, Benjamin. 2001. *Democracy in Divided Societies: Electoral Engineering for Conflict Management.* Cambridge: Cambridge University Press.

Riaz, Ali and Subho Basu. 2010. *Paradise Lost? State Failure in Nepal.* New Delhi: Adarsh Enterprises.

Roy, Asha Narayan. 2003. "Communities-Civil Society and Conflict Management". In Raoul Blendenbacher and Arnold Koller (eds.) *Federalism in a Changing World*. London: McGill-Queen's University Press. 325-336.

Sadik, Nafis. 2003. "Federalism, Decentralization and Conflict Management". In Raoul Blendenbacher and Arnold Koller (eds.). *Federalism in a Changing World*. London: McGill-Queen's University Press. 342-348.

Saunders, Cherl.2003 "Federalism, Decentralization and Conflict Management in Multicultural Societies". In Raoul Blendenbacher and Arnold Koller (eds.) *Federalism in a Changing World*. London: McGill-Queen's University Press. 33-38.

Sharma, Priyag Raj. 1997. "Nation Building, Multi-Ethnicity and the Hindu State". In David N. Gellner et al (eds.) *Nationalism and Ethnicity in a Hindu Kingdom: The Politics of Culture in Contemporary Nepal*, Amsterdam: Harwood Academic Publisher.

Smith,Graham. 2000. "Sustainable Federalism, Democratization, and Distributive Justice". In Will Kymlicka and Wayne Norman (eds.) *Citizenship in Diverse Societies*. Oxford: Oxford University Press. 345-365.

Suberu, Rotimi. 2006. "Federalism and the Management of Ethnic Conflict: The Nigerian Experience". In David Turton (ed.). *Ethnic Federalism*. Oxford: James Currey Ltd. 65-92.

Text of Comprehensive Peace Accord, 2006

Thurer, Daniel. 2003. "Federalism and Foreign Relations". In Raoul Blendenbacher and Arnold Koller (eds.) *Federalism in a Changing World*. London: McGill-Queen's University Press. 26-32.

UNDP. 2009. *Nepal: Human Development Report 2008.* Kathmandu: UNDP/Nepal

Weiner, Myron. 1978. *Sons of the Soil: Migration and Ethnic Conflict in India*. Princeton: Princeton University Press.

About the Contributors

Baral, Lok Raj (Ph.D.) is Professor & Executive Chairman of Nepal Centre for Contemporary Studies (NCCS), Kathmandu, Nepal. He served as Professor and Chairman of Political Science Department at Tribhuvan University during 1976-89. He has twenty books to his credit (both authored and edited), contributed articles and chapters in different international, national journals and edited books on Nepal and South Asia. He is also the editor of Journal of Contemporary Studies published by the NCCS and is on the advisory boards of various International journals.

Professor Baral has headed many organizations such as President of Nepal Political Science Association, Nepal Council of World Affairs, and Society for Constitutional and Parliamentary Exercises (SCOPE). He was a member of the delegation to the United Nations General Assembly in 1990, International Research Committee member of Regional Centre for Strategic Studies (RCSS, Colombo), and Nepal's Ambassador to India in 1996-97. He has lectured in India, China, Bangladesh, Pakistan, Sri Lanka, Sweden, Singapore, Japan, South Korea, USA, South Africa, UK, Germany, Norway, The Netherlands and Denmark. Professor Baral was a visiting professor at the University of Illinois at Urbana-Champaign (USA), and Fellow at CHR.Michelsen Institute at Bergen, Norway.

Edrisinha, Rohan taught at the Faculty of Law, University of Colombo, Sri Lanka, specializing in Constitutional Law. He is also a founder Director and Head of the Legal Division, Centre for Policy Alternatives, an independent public policy institute engaged in research and advocacy on conflict resolution, constitutional and law reform, human rights and governance related issues. With a degree of LL.B from University of Colombo and LL.M from University of California, Berkeley, he taught at the Faculty of Law, University of the Witwatersrand, South Africa-1995. He was a Visiting Fellow, Centre for the Study of World Religions, Harvard Divinity School. He was an unofficial advisor to the Chief Government negotiator, the Minister of Constitutional Affairs, during the peace talks between the Government of Sri Lanka and the LTTE in 2003/4 and attended the last

3 rounds of talks during that period. He is currently holding a position of International Management for UNDP/Nepal's programme entitled Support for Participatory Constitution Building in Nepal (SPCBN).

Hachhethu, Dr. Krishna is Professor of Political Science and a faculty member of Central Department of Political Science, Tribhuvan University, Kathmandu, Nepal. He is author of one dozen books, including Party Building in Nepal (2002), Nepal in Transition (2008), State Building in Nepal (2009), and has credit of publishing more than five dozen articles in books and journals published in Nepal and abroad. He was visiting scholar to Oxford University in 2005. He is former member of High Level Commission of State Restructuring of Nepal. Prof. Hachhethu is country coordinator of South Asia Democracy Study network. He has experiences of working with international organizations, i.e. International IDEA, DEFID, UNDP, NORAD on several subjects like democracy, political party, governance, election, state restructuring etc.

Khan, Dr. Abdur Rob a former Research Director at the Bangladesh Institute of International and Strategic Studies (BISS), is currently Associate Professor of International Relations at North South University, Dhaka. With a PhD in International Relations from the University of Kent at Canterbury, Dr. Khan specializes in security and conflict studies. He is the author of numerous articles in professional journals and edited volumes. He also edited a number of books on security of small states, non-traditional security and BIMSTEC cooperation. His publications include Human Security Index for South Asia.

Khanal, Krishna P. is Professor of Political Science. He is currently a Director of the UNDP/Nepal's programme entitled Support for Participatory Constitution Building in Nepal (SPCBN). He is author/editor of about six books and has also credit of publishing several articles on democracy, governance and federalism. Professor Khanal was also the Executive Director of Centre for Nepal and Asian Studies, Kathmandu, and advisor to Prime Minister , G.P.Koirala.

Mohapatra, Dr. Bishnu N. is Professor at Azim Premji University, Bangalore, India. Formerly taught Politics at the Centre for Political Studies at Jawaharlal Nehru University and University of Delhi, India. Held visiting faculty positions at University of Kyoto, Japan and National University of Singapore. He headed the governance portfolio of the Ford

Foundation's South Asia office at New Delhi from 2002-2010. Bishnu is a well-known Indian poet who writes in Odia.

Siddiqa, Dr. Ayesha is a graduate of King's College Londonwhere she did her PhD in War studies in 1996. She has written extensively on Pakistan military and her research has covered issues varying from Pakistan military's covert development on military technology, defensive game theory, nuclear deterrence, arms procurement, arms production to civil-military relations in Pakistan.She was the 'Pakistan Scholar' at the Woodrow Wilson International Center for Scholars at Washington, D.C. for 2004-05. Dr. Siddiqa is also an author, and her books include, Pakistan's Arms Procurement and Military Buildup, 1979-99: In Search of a Policy (2001) and Military Inc.: Inside Pakistan's Military Economy (2007).

Index

Samiti (PCJSS) 84, 85, 89, 90, 91

PML-N 58, 60, 65, 69, 74

PML-Q 65, 69, 73

Pourashavas 79, 82

President Kumaratunga 103, 104, 105, 108, 111, 167

President Rajapakse 94, 104, 108, 109, 110, 111, 112, 168

Prevention of Terrorism Act 38

Prime Minister Ranil Wickremasinghe 104, 105, 111, 169

Pushtoon 10, 56

R

Rahim Yar Khan 57, 68

Rajat Ganguly 13

Ram Chandra Guha 24

Rangamati Hill District Council Act 86

Rashtriya Jana Morcha 114, 124

Rashtriya Janamukti Party 121, 127, 168

Ratnasiri Wickremanayake 104

Rohan Edrisinha v, 11, 13, 94, 168

S

Sadbhabana Party 121, 127, 168

Samajwadi Prajatantrik Party 127, 168

Saraiki 10, 54, 55, 58, 59, 60, 61, 62, 63, 64, 65, 66, 67, 68, 69, 72, 74

Saraiki Province 59

Sarkaria Commission 50

Scheduled Castes 25

Scheduled Tribes 25

Shanghiya Loktantrik Rashtriya Munch 127, 169

Shanti Bahini 77, 83, 84, 85

Sharchok 22

Soulbury Constitution 97

South Asian Association of Regional Cooperation (SAARC) 20, 22, 24, 111, 169

T

Taliban 21, 34

Tamshaling 154

Tarai-Madhes Lokatantrik Party 127, 169

Telengana 45

Telugu Desam Party 50

Terrorist and Disruptive Activities Prevention Act 38

Thirteenth Amendment 99, 100, 101, 102, 103, 104, 106, 110, 111

Concurrent List (List III) 101

Provincial Councils (List I) 101

Reserved List (List II) 101

Treaty of Sugauli 19

U

Unified Communist Party of Nepal (Maoist) (UCPNM) 120, 127, 130, 131, 133

www.ingramcontent.com/pod-product-compliance
Lightning Source LLC
Chambersburg PA
CBHW070810300326
41914CB00078B/1930/J